For  Gail Stanley

THE MEADS OF LOVE

best wishes

Paul Neuner

7/10/95

" the ineffable grief
of the laughing banana "

JOHN HARRIS.

THE MEADS
OF LOVE

The Life and Poetry of John Harris
(1820–84)

Farewell my beautiful!
Thy sinless spirit is with Christ above:
Thou hast escaped the evils of the world:
We have a daughter in the meads of love.

Paul Newman

DYLLANSOW TRURAN

ISBN 185 022 068 9

/002065864

Published by Dyllansow Truran - Cornish Publications
Trewolsta, Trewirgie, Redruth 216796

T

Typeset by Kestrel Data, Exeter
Printed in Great Britain by Short Run Press Ltd, Exeter

"Through native genius he still achieved, against all odds, a body of poetry as fine as any but that of the half-a-dozen great poets of the Victorian age. For almost a century he has been lost to sight, destroyed, or reduced to Women's Institute status, by the bad poems that were once most praised. Now that he comes to us afresh as the poet who gave words to the energy of 19th century Cornwall, we should not willingly let him die."

D.M. Thomas
Introduction to *Songs from the Earth*, a selection of Harris's poems, 1977.

"Whether dealing with scenes of childhood, the wild life of his Cornish countryside, or the grinding drama of life of the poor – Harris captures, with marvellous economy, the explosive charge contained in the sudden moment of revelation."

Charles Causley
Times Literary Supplement, 1978

For Pam

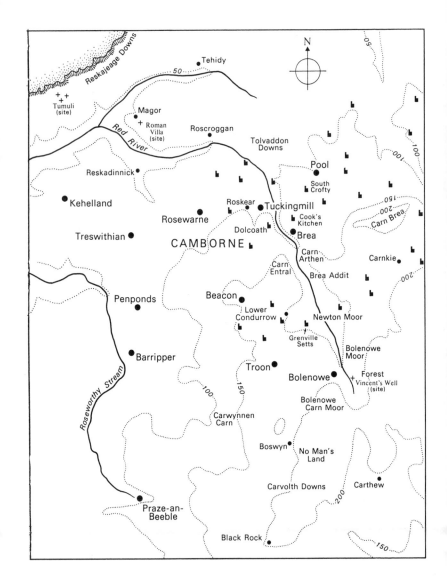

John Harris Country
(from a map by Rodney Fry)

Contents

List of Poems

Foreword

by Professor Charles Thomas

Those who come across the writings of John Harris either revel in them, or dismiss them as doggerel; there seems to be no middle way. Other poets of today, natural sympathies apart, tend to see at once the nucleus – product of a true poetic voice – that is surrounded by humdrum outpourings. But the same could be said of a great many poets, before or after Harris, whose names are far better known and who were anthologised long before *he* was. Our knowledge of Harris the man has been drawn from his own short autobiography (1882), the later and derivative *John Harris, the Cornish Poet* by his son James Howard Harris, and (for those who ever see such a rare item) *John Harris, the Cornish Poet: a lecture on his life and works*, written in 1882 and published around 1884 by his admirer John Gill, the pacifist printer from Penryn. The conventional picture that these sources give (and in the late Victorian milieu were meant to give) is of triumph over adversity, the proper use of a God-given talent, and at the end a measure of both earthly and heavenly reward. The real, the raw, the historical picture unintentionally presented, and in potentially much more detail, is of a 19th century Cornwall that came to an end between the Boer and Great Wars. Very few people under sixty, brought up in Cornwall's mining districts, could now recognise any of this; nobody else would. Harris, who died in his mid-60's, lived statistically much longer than most men who from boyhood worked as hard rock miners underground. It is just not thinkable today that any Briton could fail to find instant access to paper and pencil of some sort, or be deprived of the joys of a public library system that is or should be the envy of the civilised world (a system for which, incidentally, we can in large part thank another Cornishman, Passmore Edwards; noting, too, that Cornwall invented the scheme of inter-library loans).

John Harris's physical background – itself, central to almost everything he wrote – must be equally unfamiliar to today's readers. The remarkable aspect of the poems inspired by his visit to Kynance Cove, a beauty spot on the Lizard peninsula, and to the Land's End, is two-fold; born and raised in a maritime county, Harris rarely saw the sea, close up, until he was an adult, and when he did so it was accepted as a God-given treat and not an expected and everyday occurrence in a Cornishman's life. This, curiously, rings true and is probably supported by other under-privileged lives in the last century. Just as the poverty-ridden Swiss peasants never saw any reason to venture above the snow-line, let alone to build a national industry upon their main national asset, until excited to do so by late-Victorian visitors from Britain and other countries, so did the Cornish ignore their coast and beaches. At ports and harbours, small boys during the summer might bathe (invariably naked; no one bothered about costumes), but the corporate notion of the sea was as a source of fish and as a medium of easy transport, thought at all times a vast and basically dangerous phenomenon. Children inland seldom visited the coast and like most fishermen could rarely swim a stroke. Formal sea-bathing began as a facility for invalids like 'ozone'; from the eighties and nineties, until the Great Western Railway took over and invented the Cornish Riviera, the English middle classes started to introduce a concept of the seaside that had a most limited local following.

Harris's appreciation of the coast was at once of its natural grandeur. He may have paddled. At home he and other children paddled in ditches and streams because for most of the year they went barefoot. His home, extended only by walks to the mine and walks to visit or to work with relatives, was an economic prison. This cannot be too strongly emphasised, along with the (to us, perhaps shocking) fact that such an idea cannot have crossed his mind and that it was in any case a prison that he loved. The term 'nature poet' is actually so loose as to mean little, but if one substitutes 'poet of place', Harris was that *par excellence*. This has hitherto partly obscured a modern appreciation of the man and his work, also partly blocked some potential earlier studies. The main outpouring, the poetry from his youth and early manhood, was confined by too many restrictions. He had to turn to scratching on slate with a nail; he had minimal access to anything approaching English literature; he was forced to develop his own vocabulary, lexical and stylistic; a genuine faith had to be couched in the crude exegesis of contemporary Methodism, mainly as uttered by local preachers; and Harris could only describe what he had encountered. The work-place, the mine, was a daily ordeal from which he escaped at dusk. The home, experienced throughout the calendar – and few poets convey, as he did, such a rich and intense identification with the seasons of each year – was his primary reservoir.

John Harris came from Bolenowe, still a small village on the high ground, the spine of Cornwall, up behind the former mining town of Camborne. Two of Harris's most ardent champions of the last few decades, the poet and novelist D.M. Thomas and myself, actually share this background. D.M. Thomas's family is linked to Carnkie, the next hamlet eastward, and my own began as small-holders and miners in Bolenowe after the Civil War moving downhill (to Camborne) and economically upward in the early 19th century. I used to suspect, and now am sure, that in my own case (and probably in that of Don Thomas, too) we stand emotionally too close to Harris and to his setting. This has not precluded tributes, a share in reviving interest, lectures and (as with D.M. Thomas's edited collection, *Songs from the Earth*) a proper and heartfelt presentation from a fellow-poet. It does rule out the pair of us, and probably quite a lot of other Cornishmen, as objective biographers. When I read many of Harris's Bolenowe poems (and I read them in the worn copies that are the subscription copies of my great-great-grandfather Charles Thomas) they are not poems by a Victorian miner, but earlier and vivid impressions of remote and private nooks that I first saw as a boy on a bicycle. When I try to follow Harris' agonised feelings in the, not a few, poems that centre upon Young Love and Rejected Proposals, my picture is of the un-named girl – my great-grandfather's cousin Eliza Thomas of Treslothan, who herself wrote poetry and died young, and would not leave her widowed mother to be Mrs Harris. When D.M. Thomas sees Harris's poems about the Camborne mines and miners, he is not primarily struck by their economic or sociological significance. The vanished mining industry is a burden, and a symbol, that a decreasing number of true Cornish men and women must carry always. Don Thomas's early response is his fine poem *The Shaft* (1973), of which he wrote 'The shaft in the poem is one and many . . . myself, my father, dead miners related to me.' And finally when I see John's first notebook – a bound quarto that he bought in September 1841 – and realise how that purchase probably swallowed up a week's free income, I have to think also with shame about the acres of paper, coppices of pens and pencils and several miles of typewriter ribbon taken for granted over forty years.

I hope these words explain the pleasure with which I opened the script of this study *The Meads of Love*. At the beginning I had guessed, and at the close was convinced, that in Paul Newman the Cornish poet John Harris has at last found his proper biographer. Mr Newman combines, as so rarely happens, total empathy with his subject, a certain and welcome detachment in literary criticism, and the impressive outcome of a lot of hard work. For his book is not simply literary criticism on its own; it is quite possible to churn that out (as unkind persons said about David Hume's *History of England*) lying upon a sofa and being disinclined to get up to check facts. Harris's life, which happens to be reasonably well-documented both explicitly and implicitly, forms part of Victorian history. All good historians know that there is really no such thing as 'national history'; national history has to be the sum of all possible local histories, and they are the most demanding tasks to pursue. Paul Newman's objectivity, the essential wider setting that he provides, the quantity of new and as far as I can see hitherto unrecorded information, and the felicity of his prose, all come together to give us the kind of biography that I would have loved to have written myself – except that I probably could not, and certainly would not have done a tenth so well.

Why bother about John Harris? Because he is still worth bothering about, and will be as long as anyone can read his better poems and wonder how, despite such a host of obstacles, he found the means to give us what welled up within him. Harris has never, fortuitously, received the exposure accorded to John Clare, with whom inevitably people tend to match him. The background to his life is actually more interesting than Clare's, but has it been previously set out? In 1984, on January 7th, the centenary of Harris's death at Falmouth, three of us met in Treslothan churchyard, by the grave of the poet and of his beloved little daughter Lucretia – the present incumbent (Francis Sutcliffe), with Richard Henry Thomas and myself as the current representatives of two out of the four Bolenowe families so closely linked to John in his life-time. We laid a wreath of bay-leaves, the correct honour to give a poet. Paul Newman's wreath, in the shape of this book, took much longer to create; it will endure much longer, too; and, in thanking him for allowing me to introduce it, I want to record the delight that it has brought me and the certainty that many, many, other people will welcome it equally.

MY AUTOBIOGRAPHY

BY

JOHN HARRIS.

WITH A PHOTOGRAPHIC PORTRAIT OF THE AUTHOR.

LONDON:
HAMILTON, ADAMS, AND CO.
FALMOUTH: THE AUTHOR.   PENRYN: JOHN GILL AND SON.
EXETER: F. CLAPP, ROSENEATH, ST. JAMES'S ROAD.
1882.

Title page of Harns autobiography (1882)

JOHN HARRIS

[1820–1884]

Carn Brea

How the great mountain like a rocky king
Stands silent in the tempest! Not a gust
With water laden, rushing with fierce front
Against his wrinkles, but he shakes it off,
Like filmy atoms from an insect's wing.
The thunder growls upon his splinter'd head,
Yelling from cave to cave, and every crag,
Carved by the Druid in the olden time,
When men were wont to worship on his crest,
Seems like a fiery pillar, as the flames
Leap from the clouds, and lick their knotty sides.
He, awful in his calmness, shakes his locks,
And gazes up into the solemn sky,
As if a strain of music shook the air.
O wondrous mountain, 'neath thy ribs of rock
Lie beds of precious mineral, which, when Time
With tardy feet hath crept through other years,
Shall cheer the seeker with their shining store.
Rude ridge of boulders, carn of polish'd crag!
Eternal utterer of the Deity,
I muse within thy shadow, and look up,
As on the face of the Invisible,
And sounds rush from thee in the tempest's clang,
And rattle round the portals of my soul,
Like oracles from the eternal hills;
And I have thought in childhood, when my feet
First press'd the mosses that hang down thy sides,
And bore me wondering 'mid thine isles of rock,
That on a night of tempest, wild and weird,
The Man i' the Moon had tumbled boulders down,
Which, rolling rudely, raised thee, root and rib.
I need no other monitor to show
The impress of Jehovah. Thou art full
Of the Eternal, and His voice is heard
Among the Druid temples of Carn Brea.

Introduction

The purpose of this book is to effect a modification in the present canon of English poetry which has always excluded the Cornish poet John Harris from the Victorian pantheon, while providing space for minor writers like R.S. Hawker, William Johnson Cory, T.E. Brown, Alice Meynell, Dowson and others. Harris's best work has a concentrated power and tension and deserves to be brought before an English-speaking audience; to be read at schools and colleges and included in any anthology of Victorian poetry that may appear in the future.

I first picked up a second-hand copy of Harris's *Monro* over seven years ago, while browsing in a Clevedon bookshop. It was decorated with small, almost touchingly simple engravings, the work of the poet's invalid son, Alfred. I read the book with some interest, but it was not until later, when I came across his elegy on the death of his daughter, Lucretia, and the stunning and terrible lines beginning, "Hast ever seen a mine?", that I realised he was a poet of genius.

D.M. Thomas, the poet and novelist, came across Harris's writings around 1970. A Cornish publisher had asked him to make an anthology of poems about the Duchy, advising him to have a look at Harris, "the miner-poet from Camborne." Thomas spent a couple of days in Redruth Library, skimming through various titles, and then picked up a volume of Harris's and was straightway impressed by "A Shakespearian kind of concreteness and Romantic vision" that "seemed together to be at work energising an Augustan vocabulary." He concluded that the key to Harris's writings was his joy, his "quiet radiance" and ability to create tone-poems as in music.

Harris, indeed, has a message for us today, a capacity that has been lost or forgotten: to absorb and transmute into praise the hard lessons of life. His values are domestic and altruistic: honesty, hard work, caring and spreading the Gospel. He seems so upright and pious as to have little in common with modern poets, several of whom have found it necessary to escape from their craft into drink. With Harris it was the opposite: he spurned the gin-shops to escape into his poetry. His life was so harsh that any vacillation might have proven fatal. He could not enjoy the luxury of falling apart. But there is always common ground between poets, and when Dylan Thomas stated that he wrote "for the love of Man and in praise of God," Harris would have surely agreed.

Donald Rawe of the Lodenek Press brought out a collection of Harris's poems in 1977, entitled *Songs from the Earth* with introduction and editing by D.M. Thomas. His choice of poems was bold and radical, including most of *Carn Brea*, all of *Kynance Cove*, the first part of *Land's End* as well as fragments of "ore" from shorter poems. But save for a brief extract, one of Harris's best long poems *Monro* was excluded, along with other pieces of incidental interest. This volume, which was only brought out in a small edition, is now virtually unobtainable, so I think it is timely to make another selection, containing many of D.M. Thomas's preferences as well as my own.

As Harris's life was an interesting one, inextricably bound up with his poetry, I have written a compact biographical study, basing my information upon his 1882 autobiography, his son's bio- graphy, Professor Charles Thomas's fascinating booklet and the collected works. Tracing Victorian families is not a simple business. Christian names are passed from father to son down through the generations which can create the effect of being lost in an Ionesco drama where every character is called John. Fortunately I was guided expertly through a labyrinth of dates and relationships by Arthur Langford of Redruth, great-nephew of John Harris, grand- son of Mark Harris. Not only did he read my manuscript twice, he corrected errors with detailed notes and told me about the later history of the family in America.

Also of inestimable help was Professor Charles Thomas who kindly shared his knowledge of Bolenowe families, sending me printed matter and throwing in intriguing clues and suggestions. He too overhauled the manuscript, excising at least one major confusion, then adding notes on subjects as varied as Harris's nomenclature, the Camborne Quaker, John Budge, Robert Burns, the Thomas sisters and the spiritual and physical geography of 19th century Bolenowe. As if this was not expansive enough, he drew my attention to suitable publishers and contributed a masterful introduction. For my own part, I make no pretence of having written a work of scholarship – much of the difficult spadework has been done by others – but I hope that this biographical profile will prove useful. For I am convinced that one's appreciation of the poems is enlarged by knowing details of the life of this extraordinary miner, who, in defiance of poverty, hardship and exploitation, fashioned verses as crystalline and permanent as the granite boulders strewn across the landscape of his childhood.

Chapter One

Bolenowe – The early years

Six Chimneys is a sturdy, modernised building. In 1840 it consisted of a row of five cramped cottages which may have had an extra chimney. Partly demolished today, it retains its name and magnificent outlook, perched high up in the hamlet of Bolenowe in the hill country south of Camborne. Not far away rises the nine-mile long Red River whose romantic name derives from mineral effluent. The solitary homestead looks across the valley to the ragged outline of Carn Brea and the Basset Memorial (1836), a renowned landmark erected to honour Francis Basset, Lord Dunstanville of Tehidy, "great and good man, Nobleman, Patriot and a Christian, Philanthropist, the benefactor, the friend and advisor of the poor." Such a lofty obelisk might appear almost arrogantly assertive for someone who embodied all those Christian virtues, but it must have impressed itself upon the imagination of another Christian gentleman, less materially endowed than Francis Basset, but possessed of a more lasting and original gift.

I refer to the poet John Harris, who was born at Six Chimneys, 14th October, 1820, the year when Keats brought out his third volume of poetry and George III died mad. He was the son of John and Kitty Harris who had married earlier that year and moved to their new home near the summit of Bolenowe Carn. The hamlet lay outside the mining districts of Camborne and Redruth, then one of the richest sources for tin and copper in the world. The prosperity was superficial, however. For the miners, the wages were meagre, twelve to fifteen shillings a week, and the trade suffered fluctuations of supply and demand.

John Harris Senior, like many of his peers, supplemented his wages by farming a seven-acre smallholding which he held on lease. A dour, uncomplaining man, who embodied the Methodist virtues of hard work and regular Bible-reading, he once took the young John Harris for an evening ramble. The sky was clear and the stars were coming out. Taking his son's hand, he led him up to the crest of the hill. From that tranquil patch of earth, the boy felt that he could reach out and touch the heavens, an experience that he was to recall in his autobiography with undimmed rapture:

'*The firmament was covered with stars . . . How brightly they beamed in their mystic orbits in the blue deeps of ether. The universe looked like a bright palace of gems, where angels banqueted at the table of love . . . Suddenly my father in a soft and solemn voice, befitting the majesty of the moment, exclaimed, 'God is author of all this, my son. He made the stars also.'*

This view was conveyed to the boy at an early age and during an era which was relatively uncluttered by astronomy and planetary data. Young John Harris was to cling to this concept – his subsequent career was a devout chronicle of labour and praise. Born in a naked-raftered cottage of rough granite boulders crowned by a thatched roof, through which, after rough weather, the stars could be seen, his perceptions were God-inspired from the start.

One of his earliest memories was of the little white coffin in which his baby sister was carried to the grave, impressing upon his mind images of mortality, of the transience of life and the rapacity of death. He was the oldest and most bookish of all the Harris children (ultimately there were seven sons and three daughters). None of his immediate family understood the extraordinary fervour of his literary inclinations; some were even contemptuous of readers and dreamers. His grandmother, Joan, kept goats rather than books; his grandfather on his father's side, Ben Harris, a tall old man who wore a wide-brimmed hat and a Quaker-cut coat, was once lent by a neighbour a copy of *Paradise Lost*. He promptly returned the volume with the remark – "The man who wrote that ought to be hanged." Ben's standard reaction to any kind of reproof was the pithy – "Thee show me a man without a fault, and I will show thee a man without a head."

Six Chimneys lacked a back door and windows on the north side, save for a tiny one in the pantry. The eastern wall had once been almost blown apart by Matthew Harris, the poet's uncle, who had the rousing notion of attempting to dry a bag of wet gunpowder beside the fire. But such incidents only added to the stock of family legends which enriched the poet's early youth. John portrays his boyhood as a country idyll. His home was a haven of shining pewter plates, dresser-shelves and well-sanded clay floors. Meals consisted of vegetables, potato-cake, pasties and pilchards, and he ate to the sound of a furze fire, knitting needles and larks floating in the sunshine.

Early on in life, John was taught to kneel and pray. "And then," he recalled, "come picture books and toys, marbles and trundling hoops, and anon Little Red Riding Hood, Goody Two Shoes, Jack the Giant Killer, Sally Meanwell, Fifth of November, and then the green satchel and away to the village school."

In fact, Harris's parents were too poor to afford books or toys, or anything inessential to their precarious livelihood. Instead they kept pigs and a well-tended vegetable patch, yielding a supply of potatoes and turnips for the winter. Every Sunday his father led him along a path which ran through meadows, in summer all abrim with butterflies, humming bees and flowers. Finally they reached Troon chapel where the serious business began. He nostalgically recalled those early church-going walks:

> The Gothic window where I sit
>   Looks out upon the moor,
> And Autumn's hand has thickly strewn
>   The dry leaves at our door.
> But o'er the hills I dimly see
>   Another golden morn,
> My father led me by the hand
>   Through fields of waving corn.

In the evening, around the fire, his mother, Kitty Harris, would charm him with tales of Christian triumph and fortitude. She would tell him how honest humility was raised up and ignoble pride trampled down, how false values disguised themselves as virtues

3

and how hallowed deeds were often performed in secret. She pitted high-principled beggars against depraved but immaculately clad men of the world, emphasising that piety was better than mere prosperity. These bold, naive contrasts had a powerful influence on the youthful Harris – all of his subsequent writings contain an element of sermonising.

Local folklore played a part in their lives. John heard about Giant Bolster with his unfeasibly long stride, and of the crock of guineas which lay hidden under the stones at Hangman Barrow. When five years old, he strayed from his house and played among the daisies and clover, until the sun dropped and he could not find his way back. He walked round and round in circles, until his parents found him sobbing and saying, "There is nobody here but I and the Buckaw." The Buckaw was a malign spirit who haunted the neighbourhood.

Parish feasts were eagerly looked forward to by the children and they were held on the nearest Sunday to November 11th. John's uncle, George Smith, came along and joined in. A flute-playing bachelor with a fondness for drink, he might well have swelled the ranks of the Wise Men of Gotham. Allegedly he once mistook the moon shining in a large insanitary horse-pond outside his house for the white linen of his bed. Sliding off his horse, he curled up comfortably in the vile liquid, then jumped out and screamed his mishap to the neighbourhood.

Among John's favourite relatives on his father's side was Granny Joan who grew herbs and kept goats. With her red cloak and frizzed hair, her friendly cat and knitting needles, he saw her as the epitome of kindness. She would treat him to sweets and heavy potato-cake and he eventually memorialised her in verse.

A sadder memory was of the time when John Harris Senior was forced to take up the rod and apply it to his eldest child. His expression was mournful and severe as he took John into the stone-paved court and chastised him in full view of the bickering sparrows on the thatch. Such painful, humiliating experiences were blotted out by happier memories, such as the day when his father took him and brother William to the sands of Gwithian. "I shall never forget the impression made upon my mind," he wrote, "when I first drew near the great ocean, beheld the huge cliffs and rocks, and heard the thunder of billows upon the shore. I saw it afterwards in my dreams, and heard its eternal roll among the daisies and lark-bursts of my mountain meads."

In those days education was not compulsory. Poor folk were anxious to see their offspring working and earning. Except at the higher seats of learning, the profession of teaching was not honoured in rural districts. A modicum of literacy was all that was required to become a tutor at a country school. John Harris's first teacher was Dame Trezone, an old lady with red hair and a penchant for snuff-taking.

Young John mastered the alphabet and reading quickly, for which attainments his father presented him with a penny abridgement of *Robinson Crusoe* with a pictorial frontispiece. From Dame Trezone's establishment, he was sent to the more advanced school in Troon Chapel run by Dame Penpraze, and then to a harsher institution run by a man called Reed, who was small-eyed, bald and ferocious. He regularly caned boys with a flat piece of wood studded with sharp nails which inevitably drew blood. This method of correction appalled and terrified the sensitive boy. He begged his parents to find him another school, which they did, an academy set in a thatched house by the roadside at Forest Gate. It was run by a one-legged ex-miner called Roberts, whose teaching began and finished with an extempore prayer. Though ignorant of geography, history and any literature save the *Bible*, Roberts was a far more compassionate teacher than Reed and was able to imbue the children with a working knowledge of the three R's.

At Roberts' school, John made early experiments in writing verse. But he had scant opportunity to develop this talent, for when he was nine, he left school to work for his "uncle", George Harris of Bolenowe. Farmer George was 75 years of age at the 1841 census. As the poet's grandfather was not married until 1774, George could not have been brother to the poet's father. Therefore one may interpret "uncle" as a courtesy title to a distant relative. In appearance, George was a tall, bony man with grey eyes "who had more faith in the ghosts of the beacon than the virtue of books." Along with the two horses, Bob and Fly, John would plough the fields, cut the turf and watch his unfastidious uncle, attired in a blue frock, dispatch pigs to the afterlife. The poet was kept too busy to jot down rhymes, nor could he remember the prudent farmer paying him any wage, save a daily dinner of cold meat and roast potatoes.

The work with Uncle George did not last long and, after a few months, he became assistant to an old tin-streamer named Waters, who searched for alluvial or lode outcrops of copper and tin. It was hard work with a quality of excitement about it – one might always strike rich – and Harris learned to distinguish minerals by their colours and signs:

> Copper has colours different in the ores,
> As various as the rainbow – black and blue
> And green and red and yellow as a flower;
> Gold-coloured here, there dimly visible . . .
> Tin is more secret far, with duller eye
> Oft hiding in the river's shingly bed,
> Or the flint's bosom, near the central fires,
> In chambers wide, or veins like silken lace . . .

Tin-streaming was the traditional method of extracting ore from the surface deposits. Waters would find a favourable situation, usually along the side of a valley, and then, taking out a lease or set with the landowner, he would sink a deep hatch or shaft on to the rocky shelf or clay bed where the tin gravel lay. At best it was arduous pick and shovel toil, said to develop those broad shoulders which made a Cornish regiment take up more room on a parade ground than any other. Old workings would be sifted through, and one day John and Waters found a Jew's House in a bog – a mass of tin which had spilled over the smelting-pot and sunk. The metal was loaded up and carted to Hayle where Waters received the sum of £37.

*

At the age of ten, John became a full-time miner. He left Waters and was employed as a surface-worker at Dolcoath Mine, Camborne, where he treated the copper drawn up from the depths. There he saw young men with ore-stained red jackets and bonneted girls or "bal-maidens" hard at work, wheeling barrowloads of stone, breaking it down with hammers in the cobbing houses, and sorting out the good ore at the picking-tables.

An author of the period, Dr Paris, visited Dolcoath and observed all the activity from the brow of the hill. "Steam engines," he wrote, "Water wheels, Horse whims and Stamping mills were all to be seen in motion, together with many hundred labourers busily engaged in separating, dressing and carrying ore. A stream of water turned numerous wheels and served various other purposes in its course."

Dr Paris viewed this with "surprise and exultation." The workers found things less uplifting. While his father descended into the depths of Dolcoath, John lugged about ore-laden barrows in the heat of the sun and the clamminess of the Cornish drizzle. The work ran against the grain of his character, yet he managed to sustain himself by transmuting into verse the harsh realities around him and by living inside his head. His fellow labourers noticed his pensiveness and reluctance to share their broad and bawdy jests. They began to jeer and rebuke him, but his equability and distance also prompted their curiosity.

When they discovered that he was an aspiring poet, they encouraged him to read his effusions. Here John at last succumbed to the delights of showmanship. Standing on an upturned barrow or on a stack of minerals, he spouted spontaneous rhymes while his audience smiled and clapped. These early jingles, along with their audience, have long since been interred, but they elicited such amazed exclamations as "What a wonderful boy that is! He can read a book like a parson!"

Attitudes to the young miner's verbal precocity varied. Captain James Thomas, a friendly and sympathetic neighbour, "threw open his library door" – an expansive description of what was probably a collection of Methodist journals and a few literary classics. Hugh Rogers, the rector of Camborne, loaned him Southey's *Remains of Henry Kirke White*, which he studied "with great avidity and delight." Later the rector called at Six Chimneys and glanced at some of the poet's effusions. Harris came in with sod-soiled hands and waited for the verdict. The clergyman was grave. He passed no congratulatory comment, warning Harris that the ways of the muse were those of poverty and the workhouse.

But Harris could not stop writing. Language had liberated his mind, and he jotted down rhymes compulsively. Incidents from his boyhood, pious anecdotes, family memories, farmyard duties – all were mentally hoarded and framed in stanzas. Many of his poems contain telling biographical matter, like the lines written in 1846, describing the burial of a ferret owned by his brother, William, who eventually emigrated to America to work the lead mines of South West Wisconsin. The poem was set to music and performed by child actors in 1984, for the centenary of Harris's death, in a television documentary narrated by D.M. Thomas:

Will's ferret was buried this morn:
When Samuel came down from his bed,
He whisper'd, with aspect forlorn,
"O Kitty, Will's ferret is dead."

And Kitty soon told it to Mark,
And Mark to the rest of the clan,
We sorrow'd with visages dark,
As if we were mourning a man.

So Ann made a coffin so small,
Off cast-off brown paper and thread:
This served for a shroud and a pall,
False trappings unknown to the dead.

And Samuel was sexton and clerk,
And Benjamin bearer so brave,
While Kitty, and Jacob, and Mark
Soon bore her away to the grave.

'Neath the hawthorn its grave was dug deep,
With sharp-pointed pickaxe and spade.
Lie down, little ferret, and sleep
On the couch that affection hath made.

All the other figures are Harris's brothers and sisters. Samuel Harris was born in 1833 and followed his brother to the States, becoming a mine-manager in the Michigan copper-belt and a rich man, dying in 1927. Mark Smith Harris (1841–1931) stuck to his local roots; starting out as a miner, who worked the Dolcoath man-engine, he was to develop as a versifier and an able preacher with "a natural flow of lyrical speaking." Ann Harris (1826–1910) married James Sims in Wisconsin in 1847 and died in Council Bluffs, Iowa. Christiana or Kitty Harris (1836–1901) married the widower Trevithick in 1877 but did not get on well with his children. Benjamin (born 1838) also emigrated to America, drawn along the mining trail; he became superintendent of the great copper mills at Lake Linden and of Calumet and Hecla mine in Upper Michigan; his obituary noted that "Good books had a charm for him." Jacob (born 1843) followed after him and eventually went through college in Missouri where he trained to become a minister in the Methodist Episcopal Church; he was ordained in 1870. It seems that the poet was one of the few members of the family, who did not eagerly espouse underground labour, preferring to pluck ore from his imagination.

SIX CHIMNEYS.

Six Chimneys, the birthplace of John Harris by John Alfred Harris

9

Chapter Two

Dolcoath – Twenty-five years underground

At the age of twelve Harris's youth was finished. A terrible plague of Asiatic cholera swept the land, killing nearly fifty-three thousand people. First it appeared in Sunderland, then spread throughout London and the Midlands, dispatching most of its victims within twenty-four hours. Mining communities were affected by this virulent outbreak which doctors were powerless to treat. Convulsed with violent spasms, the body would become livid, the pulse fail and death ensue.

The Duke of Buckingham said that he would prefer the cholera to the new bill before Parliament. Earl Grey, the Whig prime minister, observing the revolution in France, had stated that "we should learn wisdom from what is passing before our eyes, and when the spirit of liberty is breaking out all around, it is our first duty to secure our own institutions by introducing into them temperate reform." Amid grim Tory predictions about the impending collapse of society, the *Great Reform Bill of 1832* was passed and Britain took her first step towards full parliamentary democracy, an event marked by tar barrels being set ablaze on the chimney-top of Pednandrea mine, Redruth, and flags, bands, processions and fireworks elsewhere in the county.

But the new law, extending the franchise to rent-paying householders and other privileged factions, scarcely affected the lives of most miners who were too poor to qualify for the vote. *The Poor Law Amendment Act (1834)* made far greater impact, restricting freedom further by giving relief only in the shape of labour, and introducing an "improved" workhouse system so that, as one reactionary put it, "able-bodied paupers should become manly labourers with homes of comfort and content."

In this socially turbulent context, Harris became a miner proper, descending with his father into the pit of Dolcoath, which was over 2,000 feet deep and estimated to have some 75 miles of interconnecting passages. The journey was rickety and perilous. Ladder after ladder, ledge after ledge, all succeeding one another, had to be climbed down. A rope was attached to John, leading from his father's waist, which must have provided some comfort, as his eyes became accustomed to the netherworld.

John Harris Senior was working a passage that branched off from the main shaft. Drilling holes and laying charges, he instructed his son to load the loosened rock into a barrow and wheel it to "the plot" or place where it was collected and drawn up in buckets to the surface. Candles were attached to the ends of barrows; they flickered like gloworms as they were wheeled through the blackness. The work was full of hazards and injuries: grazing, bruising and the breaking of limbs.

No safety precautions existed then at Dolcoath. Amid the dripping heat and sulphur fumes, buckets would come crashing down from severed chains. Fragments of rock would shear off from the uneven sides and shatter on the stagings. Such accidents, coupled with the torrid atmosphere, inspired Harris to make the obvious yet telling comparison between Dolcoath and Hades. The likeness was apt enough – a pitchblack hole full of dark and sweating shapes, smoke, explosions, curses and clanging machinery. He both hated and dreaded it, yet he wrought a language appropriate to his terror.

> *Hast ever seen a mine? Hast ever been:*
> *Down its fabled grottoes, wall'd with gems,*
> *And canopied with torrid mineral-belts,*
> *That blaze within the fiery orifice?*

John had a close escape by attending a Sunday school treat. He and four other miners, including two of his brothers, had been working on a kind of sink or well, above which unknown to them were hanging bulky masses of loose rock. While he and his brothers were enjoying buns and hymns, a terrifying crash resounded through the levels of Dolcoath. The roof above the sink had collapsed – in this instance entombing nobody – but they never forgot their providential absence that day. For there were many less fortunate occasions when miners died of crushing, blasting or asphyxia.

And then there was the time when he and Uncle William were using the pick and iron wedges to cut through a lode. By mistake, Harris let his candle go out. Alarmed he turned to see Will feverishly blowing on his own wick. The glint died immersing them in pitch darkness. They were in a narrow, unfrequented part of the mine. To cry for help would be useless; the only choice they had was to crawl back through to the top of the mine. This they did, Harris leading and using the pick to test the way ahead. Inch by painful inch they ascended. They went up rock faces where small notches had been cut for the feet; crawled through low workings which cut their skin; through long levels which had deep sinks breached only by narrow planks; up long sets of ladders, shifting over as they reached the top – "A single slip of the foot, and we should be lost in some grim excavation where we might be undiscovered until the sea gave up its dead, and the earth put on its flaming funeral-shroud." Finally they saw a speck of light "like a distant star" which became larger until they felt the shock of blinding sunshine.

Poetry, as might be expected, was his sole consolation during all the grinding labour. The other miners might fill their leisure with such activities as drinking, wrestling, jumping in sacks or watching cock-fights at Camborne, but Harris shunned such raucous diversions. After a day's work, he would retire to his bedroom and compose verses, resting his paper on a pair of bellows and wrapping his feet in his mother's shawl. Eager to acquire a broad knowledge of literature, he borrowed books and saved up five shillings to buy a dictionary.

A love of nature went side by side with the poetry. He often rambled over the top of Carnmenellis, where he would gather wood anemones and admire the feathery lichen that grew on the granite pillars. Carn Brea was a favourite retreat with its castle, crags, ancient monuments and mine-stacks. This hill was to inspire Harris in the same way that Skiddaw or Helvellyn inspired the Lake poets. It became the trigger of his imagination, a mountain citadel peopled with white-robed Druids, holy men, Danes, saints, soldiers and heretics.

He almost certainly attended the laying of the foundation stone of the Carn Brea Monument, honouring the passing of Francis, Lord de Dunstanville and Basset of Tehidy. In the summer of 1836 around thirty thousand people, "a mountain of flesh," gathered on the hill and watched ten to twelve hundred miners, wearing the colours of the Pendarves family, prominent landowners of the district, march up to the summit led by the mining captains. The Provincial Grand Lodge of Cornwall attended in full, paying tribute to their Brother Freemason, and gentry, working-men and ladies with tippets brushed shoulders. The ceremony was the first step in a laborious rota of construction, and over the years the bombastic obelisk arose, like a hollow shout of grandeur.

Another far more important innovation came the following year. In 1837 the first locomotive in West Cornwall made an experimental trip over part of the road between Hayle and Camborne, with a train of waggons containing about 300 people. The coming of the railway was to revolutionise the transport of minerals in the West Country and totally alter the working-man's relation to his environment, increasing his potentiality for employment.

Meanwhile, half a mile below ground, Harris worked with slimy water lapping around his knees in unventilated passages which reeked of sulphur fumes. Perspiring, with mineral dust sticking to his skin and clothes, he bored into the rock-faces while suspended from a wooden platform – his life depending on a knot's strength. He had nowhere to rest when he reached exhaustion-point, only the rough stone floor. The water in the mine was scarcely drinkable. Harris had to suck it in through clenched teeth to avoid the maggots that bred profusely in the heat.

"Sometimes," he recalled in his autobiography, "I stood on a stage hung in ropes in the middle of a wide working, where my life depended on a single nail being driven into a plank . . . Sometimes I stood on a narrow board high up in some dark working, holding the drill, or smiting it with the mallet, smeared all over with mineral, so that my nearest friends would hardly know me, until my bones ached with the severity of my task, and the blood dropped off my elbows . . . Sometimes I had to dig through ground where it was impossible to stand upright, and sometimes to work all day, as if clinging to the face of a cliff. Sometimes I have been so exhausted as to lie down and sleep on the sharp flints, and sometimes so thirsty that I have drunk stale water from the keg . . . Sometimes I had wages to receive at the end of the month, and sometimes I had none. But I despaired not, nor turned the Nymph of Song from my side."

The shifts were long – estimated at around six hours. On finishing, Harris had to climb two thousand feet of ladders, and then, perhaps in the middle of a cold winter's night, trudge back to his cottage. If he emerged during the hours of light, he might take a quick meal and then begin evening work on his father's smallholding: fields had to be ploughed, sheep rounded up and the cow milked. Harris endured such an existence for twenty-four years and all the time the process of poetic sublimation continued. He poured out lyrics and verse narratives celebrating nature, God, domestic and celestial virtues. Lack of clean paper prompted him to resort to traditional improvisations such as grocery wrappings. Often he would scratch rhymes with his nail on smooth bits of slate, roof-tiles and iron wedges. Blackberry juice was his substitute for ink.

With such demands on his time, the poet felt the need for a sanctuary to which he could retire and taste his own solitariness or immerse himself in delighted reverie. Just as an artist requires a studio, Harris decided that a poet requires a bower as a frame to his compositions. Fortunately there was a site near his cottage which provided both the shelter and the tranquility. It comprised a wide ditch, dug up to fill in a hedge which lined a meadow. Harris would sit on a strip of turf near the base of the hedge, and there, overhung by canopies of heather and trailing plants, he would read or write poems.

"The swallows wheeled around me, floating down the hillside over gorse-brakes and thyme-banks where fays frolicked unseen, now low, now high, and then back again on their arrowy flight, so that their wings almost fanned my flowing hair. Not a sound disturbed the solitude, save the clear river in the valley, or the last lay of the lark among the crimson clouds."

One Sabbath morning, young Harris was reclining in his bower when he was approached by two young men who tried to persuade him not to attend Sunday School but to go adventuring with them. Thinking of the grief of his father, Harris declined. Soon after, he was approached by these young men again, who sought to lure him into bad company, but again he avoided involvement.

In later years, he learned that his two unholy companions had emigrated to America. "In the middle of a mighty forest," he wrote with sombre relish, "with no one near them but a lonely traveller, they were suddenly smitten with a fatal disease, dying in the darkness in the midst of the vast solitude. They were both buried in one rude grave, without tear or funeral-rite, which is now lost in the boundless wilderness; and the wild beasts prowl over their nameless tomb." What credibility one can attach to these stories is a moot point. The miner-poet's desire to wring a good sound Methodist moral from the most random of happenings sometimes becomes an obtrusive mannerism. He is prepared to sacrifice veracity in the interests of morality. "The good ended happily; the bad unhappily – that is what fiction means." Miss Prism and John Harris share a common literary theory.

Chapter Three

Methodist Roots

At the age of sixteen, a year before Princess Victoria came to the throne, Harris was made a Sunday school teacher at Troon. Later he acted as librarian and became the superintendent of another school at Black Rock in the parish of Crowan. The latter district he found uncultivated agriculturally and morally, with teenage boys and girls ignorant of the letters of the alphabet. For Harris, the Sabbath was no day of rest, but one wherein he gave religious instruction to the young, coupled with preaching in the mornings and afternoons, finishing work around ten o'clock at night.

The driving force of his life at this period was Methodism. He had been born in an area which had been spiritually revitalised by the teachings of John Wesley. Probably the preacher passed through Troon in the mid-1770's, delivering his last sermon at Gwennap Pit in 1789, an event which John Harris's younger brother, Mark Harris, recorded after receiving a first-hand account from Captain James Thomas.

Even the most impoverished seem to have been imbued with craggy pride by the new religious wave. As a child, Harris recalls his neighbour's little girl pointing to an aged crippled beggar. "Mother, can you see?" she called. The old man stopped on his crutches and replied sharply, "Can you see! Ay, and what can you see? A poor old man in a bundle of rags. I have been in places where I have seen the KING, and he never said 'Can you see?'"

The spiritual education of the young had always been emphasised by Wesley. Methodist Sunday Schools began in 1785 when the preacher commended the work of Robert Raikes in

Gloucestershire. They quickly spread to Cornwall and became for many children the foremost social outlet of the week. On Whit Monday 1839, Harris must have been present among the five hundred scholars and teachers who celebrated by drinking tea in the Camborne chapel and singing and praying. For many years, Thomas Shaw recorded, the children marched around the town led by a brass band; the girls dressed in white, the boys in clean collars, ending up at the local manse or "big house" – in this instance George Smith's residence "Trevu" – where they would be given saffron buns ten inches in diameter.

During the mid-nineteenth century, Harris's chief neighbours were the Bennattses of Camborne ("Granny Joan" was a Bennatts) and the Thomases, farmers and illustrious managing-agents of Dolcoath, who lived in a low thatched double-cottage. Nearby, at Treslothan, was George Bull's vicarage, the farm of Eliza, Sophia and Susanna Thomas and the schoolhouse where Samuel Whear taught. They were all on familiar terms and shared common religious enthusiasms in a parish where, in the words of Charles Thomas, "there was a kind of joint adherence to both Wesleyanism and Anglicanism . . ."

John Wesley rode some 225,000 miles throughout Britain, preached 40,000 sermons, taught his congregations new hymns – many composed by his brother Charles – and organised them into societies, classes and bands. His impact upon the Camborne-Redruth region was immense. Small parishes like Bolenowe were quick to yield to his influence. Cottage meetings were held from 1795 in the hamlet although an actual chapel was not established there until 1868. John Harris Senior held meetings at Six Chimneys and taught at Troon Sunday School when Harris was a mere boy.

So the background of John Harris was strictly – some might say narrowly – religious from the early days. Wesleyanism offered a practical doctrine of survival. Its philosophy was a mixture of the radical and the conservative, radical in that it dispensed with ceremony and qualifications – anyone of honest reputation who felt the spirit move him could preach – and conservative in the sense that it did not seek to break down the status quo. Emphasis was on self-help, combining the virtues of humility and dignity. In 1753 Wesley had set down "The Rules of a Helper" which contained such instructions as:

Be diligent. Never be unemployed for a moment. Never be triflingly employed. Never while away time; never spend more time at one place than is strictly necessary. Do not affect the gentleman . . . A Preacher of the Gospel is the servant of all.

Be ashamed of nothing that is not sin: not of fetching wood (if time permit), or drawing water; not of cleaning your own shoes or your neighbour's.

Be punctual. Do everything exactly at the time.

You have nothing to do but save souls.

Act in all things not according to your will but as a son of the Gospel.

These guidelines, severe and exact, helped prop up the dignity of hardworking though intensely poor folk who sought to better themselves by honest zeal and effort. Despite Wesley's honourable intentions, there was strong local opposition by the Anglican faction. The Reverend William Borlase, a noted cleric and antiquarian, was roused to anger by these intense and eloquent intruders. In place of the local parson, they had set up a new network of chapels, circuits and superintendent ministers, travelling representatives of Wesley. The established parochial structures were utilised to draw a new congregation of working folk, who found the new religion invigorating after the class-ridden structures of the Church of England.

Mining families, in particular, were drawn to Methodism. Living in confined two-roomed cottages or hovels scooped out of the hillside, the choice often lay between piety and the gin-houses and the more prudent usually opted for the former. As William Beckford observed when passing through Gwennap in 1787, "Methodism has made very rapid progress, and has been of no trifling service in diverting the attentions of these sons of darkness from their present condition to the glories of the life to come."

Also, it should be borne in mind that certain Methodist preachers were as charismatic as Wesley himself. Billy Bray, the most famous Cornish evangelist, had a vigorous, exhortatory style that captivated thousands; throughout his career he sustained a mood of almost hypnomanic joyousness. One of his favourite sayings was, "If they were to put me into a barrel, I would shout glory through the bunghole – praise the Lord!" He seemed to have been in a permanent state of ecstatic gratitude. "I can't help praising the Lord," he once said. "As I go along the road I lift up one foot and it seems to say 'Glory', and I lift up the other and it seems to say 'Amen'."

Born into a poor if devout family, John Harris tended to be less irrepressibly exultant. He had a melancholic side which tempered his capacity to celebrate. He praised his Maker constantly both in poetry and hymns, but combined the praise with much sorrowful reflection on death, retribution and atonement. His Methodism had a socially conscious side: like Billy Bray, who had also worked as a tinner, he sought to uphold the cause of poor but God-fearing workers against the treatment they received from the mineral magnates. One of his first poetical compositions, a dialogue between a workman and his master, was written shortly after a strike for extra wages by the disgruntled miners of the district. After labouring at it a whole night, he took it to the office of a Camborne printer, who, after keeping it for a long time, returned it with the cryptic comment, "I do not think it worth printing."

His first taste of printer's ink came when he wrote a dirge on the death of some miners who were accidentally killed on Carn Brea. These verses were recited to a poor blind man in the street, who proceeded to sing them to the crowd at Camborne market-place – Harris was thrilled rather than embarrassed. Another poem, printed in a Wesleyan magazine, was *The Story of Robin Redbreast*, mixing whimsy and winsomeness.

So I fluttered away, faint, hungry and weak,
The home of a good-natured poet to seek,
Crept forth to the door, hopped up on the sill,
Shook the snow-feathers off, and then knocked with my bill,
When out came the bard, and he gave me my fill.
So I sang him a song with significant look;
He nodded, and wrote it all down in his book.

Even during his youthful phase of creation, he only wrote two satirical poems. The first concerned a young schoolmaster who delivered a lecture at the village institute on the subject of phrenology. Harris dashed off a jingle "censuring the theme rather than the speaker." He entertained a few neighbours by reading it aloud. As a result, the lecturer called to hear the poem. When

Harris recited, the man flushed with rage, saying that it was a good deal worse than he had imagined, and that he would find it hard to forgive Harris, unless he destroyed the manuscript before his eyes. The poet tore his production to shreds, scattering the particles of wit to the mountain wind. His second piece concerned a dentist, "who had the hardihood to jerk out two of my teeth at a twitch, and one of them quite sound." Harris loaned the poem to a Quaker of Camborne, possibly John Budge, who read it and returned it, saying, "John Harris, I advise thee to put that piece in between the bars of the grate." And thus the fun went up in flames.

Aside from crude experiments in verse-making, this was a time of intensive study when Harris laid his poetic foundations. As a teenager, his reading included Methodist periodicals and writers like Bunyan but he had also absorbed popular works like Thomas Campbell's verse-narrative *Gertrude of Wyoming* which dealt with the destruction of a settlement in Pennsylvania by Mohawk Indians. The Spenserian stanzas of *Gertrude* convey sentimental leakage rather than tragic containment, but the verses have descriptive virtuosity, portraying Wyoming as an earthly paradise, a Garden of Eden. The rhyming scheme made its mark on Harris who was to use it effectively in his verse-autobiography. Campbell (1775–1844) was a leading literary figure: friend of Sir Walter Scott, a noted editor and critic, he is best remembered for his *Battle of the Baltic* and *Ye Mariners of England*.

Campbell's career was a spectacular success compared with Henry Kirke White (1785–1806), the son of a Nottingham butcher. He is one of those despondent footnotes in English literature. From lowly beginnings, Henry educated himself, learned Latin and Greek and wrote verses and hymns including *Oft in danger, oft in woe*. Through the efforts of well-meaning patrons, he gained entry to St John's College, Cambridge, where he died in his rooms from overwork and consumption, aged twenty-one. Southey edited his gruesomely titled *Remains* and Byron saluted his memory:

> *Unhappy White! while life was in its spring*
> *And thy young muse just shook her joyous wing,*
> *The spoiler came; and all thy promise fair*
> *Has sought the grave, so sleep forever there.*

Another idol was the Renfrewshire poet Robert Pollok (1798–1827), who escaped his humble agricultural origins and studied divinity at Glasgow University. He took holy orders and produced a Miltonic epic *The Course of Time* which sold well and was regularly reprinted. Harris was enthralled by the poem and claimed he would like to take it with him to the grave. Three hundred pages long and written in severe blank verse, *The Course of Time* was an apt choice for posthumous perusal, being full of darkness, doom and resurrection.

It seems that Pollok, like Henry Kirke White, was one of those unfortunate souls whose enthusiasm proved self-defeating, for he also over-exerted himself and died of consumption. Harris empathised with young, fervently religious poets who, after a bitter struggle, enjoyed flickering fame followed by tragic expiry. He felt closer to them than the lofty and distant geniuses of antiquity.

And, of course, grim as their fates were, they did at least partly achieve their ambitions. Kirke White's poems were published and praised in their time; so were Pollok's and Robert Bloomfield's. Their lives are sad successes rather than dismal failures and Harris was able to derive a crumb of comfort from reading about them. After all, he also was a young man with special abilities, and perhaps a latter-day Southey or Capel Lofft would print and promote him.

This hope – of emancipation from harsh physical toil – did much to sustain Harris. While breaking into the hard rock, images of beauty took root in his mind and their flowering helped to numb the pain of labour. His mind floated into a sensuous Edenic realm where he found rest and spiritual refreshment:

> *Exhausted oft, he made flints his bed,*
> *And dreamt of groves of olives far away,*
> *By dews divine and gales of gladness fed,*
> *Where sunlight glitters all the livelong day*
> *And harpers mid the trees and falling water play.*
> (Monro)

And, of course, this vision did touch a solid core of truth. When Harris emerged from the pit, the world seemed radiant and lit from within. True, he saw minestacks marching over the hills as far as the eye could see, a forest of stone trunks leaking fumes of arsenic and sulphur, but the wind eventually dispersed them and the poet could turn his back and go wandering in the reedy meadows and quiet dingles. He was forced to live in two worlds. Raised on the gusty heights of Bolenowe, he spent his time in the black and crowded depths of Dolcoath. Every day was a journey from darkness to light, from smoke and explosions to cool and moving air, from a murky inferno to the paradise of a rural cottage and loving family – a journey of violent and stunning contrasts which Harris managed to reconcile in his best poetry.

It is not surprising that he made a religion out of the open air; his favourite bird was the lark, "warbling in wonder on the spires of light", and his exultation in nature is rapt and continuous. Amid the fallen world he rambled as one through whom all good thoughts flowed. As a miner, he had to live as others told him. As a preacher, he told others how they should live. Only as a poet did he truly express himself, the free and cele-bratory spirit, whose obdurate commitment to song would never waver:

> The leer of envy may not stop his reed,
> > The loss of friends, or friendship's golden store,
> A childless hut, a face of abject need,
> > Nor e'en the black-browed, heavy workhouse door.
> In adverse blasts his muse will trill the more.
> > Earthquake and fire may not destroy his song,
> Nor wan disaster's sternest, wildest roar,
> > Where desolation swiftly stalks along,
> And he is earthward hurled his ruined shrines among.
> (Monro)

It is significant that he saw himself as a "bard". Traditionally one thinks of a bard as a performer, a singer who celebrates tales of victory and defeat; of love and death, passion and heroism. In the Celtic and Homeric traditions, a bard had a stock of phrases that might be re-used in a variety of orations in much the same way that an extempore preacher had a supply of edifying texts and forceful slogans that could be re-assembled for different con-gregations. Harris also had his favourite phrases and situations that he would recycle, usually to demonstrate a moral. To modern ears, they may seem contrived, but Harris saw them as links in his sacred armour. For he was not an ordinary work-desk poet but someone upon whom God had conferred a marvellous gift, and his singing – his poetry – was an act of gratitude. In him poetry and religion was fused. There was no question of choice. His muse was God-given.

Victorian impression of Carn Brea

Chapter Four

Carn Brea – Mount of the Druids

When Harris was not working in Dolcoath or providing religious instruction to the young, he was often to be found walking or musing around the slopes of Carn Brea. This hill has been likened to an island, a rocky mass rising 740 feet from a coastal plain, with a summit strewn with huge masses of granite boulders and slopes covered with gorse, bracken and heather. A splendid frowning eminence, ragged and slightly sinister-looking, it has three peaks: East Point crowned with the medieval castle, Carn Ley the western peak often known as Tregajorran Carn, and the central height upon which stands the vast memorial column.

To Harris Carn Brea was a veritable mountain of mystery, a wonderland of history and romance. He was familiar with the writings of William Borlase who had recorded its numerous prehistoric relics in 1754. Borlase was a distinguished cleric; he had studied the writings of William Stukeley, a brilliant if occasionally over-romantic antiquarian who, after surveying Stonehenge and Avebury, had declared them to be Druidic temples where white-robed priests brandished golden sickles and performed incantations to the moon. This picturesque interpretation, based upon the writings of the Roman authors, inspired many poets who desired to starch up their verses with quaint and curious lore. Soft primitivism was fashionable at the turn of the 18th century: echoes of it can be found in Blake and Wordsworth and a host of dimmer lights. John Harris eagerly absorbed such theories and strode across the slopes of the Carn in a daydream of distant wizardry and mysticism.

A mining scene, Carn Brea

A mining scene, Carn Brea

I gain'd the hill-top, saw its boulders bare
Some worn by time, some carved by Druid art,
Where oft perhaps the painted Briton prayed
To Thor and Woden, offering human blood,
When moral darkness filled our blessed isle . . .
(Carn Brea)

In the same way that John Clare (1793–1864), who lived in "one quarter of a narrow hut in a plain covered with stagnant pools and overhung by mists," was able to transcend physical discomfort and celebrate his surroundings, Harris rambled over the Carn, enjoying the summer sun as much as the flashlit violence of the storm. He drew comfort from solitude and had moments of mystical elation:

The holy silence of the universe
Was more to him than gathering hosts of men,
Than clothes, or food, or volume of sweet verse

25

Inscribed of old by some immortal pen.
He knew the first flower smiling in the glen,
  The hawthorn where the robin builds its nest
The summer rush-tufts waving in the fen,
  The rabbit's burrow where the great rocks rest,
And poetry rears her bower, and he was truly blest.
(Monro)

In the 19th century the Carn was a recreation ground for the weary tinner. Wild goats ranged around it – the last one was shot by a Basset gamekeeper around 1830 – and whortleberries, which were used for tart-filling, grew on its slopes. As Michael Tangye observed, it was a place where the miner "could lie in the sun and breathe the pure air, forgetting briefly the dangerous darkness of the mines situated below him at the foot of the hill. While he dozed his children played at hide-and-seek amongst the hut circles and gigantic granite boulders. They called certain rocks by their names as their parents had done before them, and looked and listened in awe as mothers recounted tales of battling giants showing them as proof the severed head of a once mighty warrior."

Here is a charming picture of a miner and his family at play. But such a vision needs to be qualified with grimmer factual data. One might assume from reading Harris that miners were principally God-fearing Wesleyans who worked hard and worshipped hard. His autobiography is very much a personal testament. It does not dwell on the blasphemy and sordidness that characterised the lives of so many of his fellow-workers.

The early tinners, who sifted for ore, lived a semi-vagrant life; they trudged around and set up rough camps by the moorland streamworks, grabbing meals where they could. But with the advent of underground mining, new towns sprang up. A more stable and family-oriented class of miners arose, who espoused the Methodist doctrine and avoided rioting and revelry. They were by no means typical, however. Chapels were far outnumbered by the kiddleywinks or beer-houses that clustered around mining communities, and under the influence of drink the behaviour of miners could be extremely brutish.

There exists an account of a group of 19th century miners marching from St Day to Redruth in order to engage in a mob fight. They came across a dog *en route* which they killed, staining their flag with the poor animal's blood. Stoning matches between rival mining factions were commonplace, and uprisings, owing to bad wages and insanitary conditions, were prevalent during the hungry 1840's, when the emigration of Cornish miners to the lead mining districts of South West Wisconsin and North West Illinois began.

Despite adverse conditions, the miners as a class were known to take pride in their appearance. *The West Briton* (1848) carried a faintly contemptuous description of a fair at Redruth, noting how most of the men were attired in fine broad cloth, and their wives "flaunting flounces." The "holes and dens" they had emerged from, the writer remarked, "more resemble pig-styes than human abodes."

The attitude is typical. Gentry did not dwell on the working conditions of the poor, preferring to sentimentalise their plight rather than act upon it. Thomas Spargo, the mining engineer and stock-broker, argued that the Lord had favoured Cornwall with mineral wealth, and it was the duty of pious investors to increase their money tenfold. He transformed the miners into noble savages, men who cheerfully shouldered their hapless burden, and found some mysterious source of affirmation in the harshness of their toil. "How monotonous their lot," he wrote, "early in the morning, in the mid-day, you may find troops of these worthy labourers quietly and lovingly going to their underground labour, as if no other work had charms for them . . . they fulfil their destiny with a patience and hopefulness that foreshadows constant good to the members of the human race."

The average Camborne-Redruth miner would have responded to such a view with a look of amazement or an expletive. He lived in what was described in 1855 as "a hungry landscape, everywhere deformed by small mountains of many-coloured refuse; traversed in narrow paths and winding roads, by streams of foul water, by screaming locomotives with hurrying trains; while wheels and whims, and miles of pumping rods, whirling and vibrating, and the forest of tall beams, make up an astonishing maze of machinery and motion."

If the lower slopes of the Carn represented the netherworld of unceasing labour, the breezy summits were the arena of the imagination. They were John Harris's "Wuthering Heights", the savage but restorative landscape in which his poetic fancies could breed and thrive. He would tread the trackways, briefly conversing with the poor folk, the lonely widows, elderly tinners and their children, who broke the soil of the harsh moorland and cultivated potatoes and turnips. *Carn Brea* provides numerous forceful portraits of the devout Cornish poor who found solace in reading the Bible as they eked out a scant existence amid the harsh terrain.

> *In a farm-cottage on the craggy cliff,*
> *Half-hid with oak and leafy sycamore,*
> *Dwelt Pitt the ploughman . . .*

The general conditions which were prevalent may be gleaned from an account of an English visitor to the region in the 1880's. His name was William H. Rideing and he seemed to be searching for evidence of "imaginative simplicity in the English peasantry . . . the insular capacity for wonderment . . ." In general, he found that he was disappointed; rural communities had become disarmingly sophisticated. Even the daughters of miners seemed neatly clothed, intelligent and capable of reading literature "of the Adolphus-Adelina sort" which they digested in penny instalments.

Below the Carn, however, he found a genuine remnant of the past, a contemporary of John Harris, an old woman bent over a pile of unmilled copper ore. Of dwarfish statute, she was hunched and wrinkled with blue-mottled skin and thin, wiry hair. Her petticoats were stained with copper-ore which she was shovelling into a small waggon which stood on a tramway. Her face had a look "of uncomplaining suffering, of unalterable gravity, of a habituated sorrow which had extinguished all possibility of a smile." When she failed to understand Rideing's question, she used the words "Please, sir?"

RIDEING: You seem to be old for such hard work.
WOMAN: Deed, sir, I don't know how old I am, but I've been at it this forty years. I'm not young any longer, that's sure.
RIDEING: Are you married?
WOMAN: No, sir, nobody would ever have me or go with me, as I was

always subject to fits – terrible they are. I still have 'em once or twice a week sometimes, always with a change in the moon.

RIDEING: How do you account for it?

WOMAN: Why, before my twenty-fourth year, I was in the service of a lady, who threw me down stairs, and that changed my blood. So, when the moon changes, I have the fits. Little can be done for them when the blood's changed.

Her wages were fourteen pence a day. She never complained – the workhouse awaited those unable to sustain the pace. Here was a character who might easily have fitted into Harris's poetic chronicle *Carn Brea*, who probably encountered the poet during one of his youthful rambles. Dour and humbly acquiescing in whatever ill-luck held in store for her, more superstitious than religious, she is the epitome of that ungrudging acceptance of fate portrayed by Harris in his voluminous writings.

Chapter Five

Eliza Thomas

In the first half of the 1840's Harris made contact with society and began to mix with those who shared his literary tastes. A Camborne tailor lent him the poems of Robert Bloomfield, which he rated highly, and later his good friend, the young Reverend George Bull, introduced him to Shakespeare's *Romeo and Juliet*, which thoroughly entranced him. "The bitters of life changed to sweetness in the cup," he wrote, "and the wilderness around me was a region of fairies . . . and over the genii-peopled heights a new world burst upon my view" – making it sound more like *A Midsummer Night's Dream*!

George Tippet Bull was born in 1815 and became the first perpetual curate at Treslothan. Educated at Trinity College, Dublin, he helped to shape the young miner's reading and encouraged him to buy books. Among Harris's first purchases were a Bible, a hymn book and the works of Shakespeare. He formed friendships with literate people and discussed religion and philosophy. As D.M. Thomas put it, "he became his own academy, buying a dictionary from a blacksmith to learn more words, listening carefully to educated speakers; above all, grabbing at poetry, the few times he could find it, as parched lips gulp at a water-flask . . ."

Obsessed with self-improvement, he made notes in his father's account book describing the curriculum he imposed upon himself, which was the very opposite of the rake's progress. The entry for August 2nd 1842 runs: "I this day resolve to devote Mondays and Wednesdays to grammar, Tuesdays to history, or such books as I may have from the (Sunday school) library, Thursdays to poetry-reading, Fridays composition, Saturdays miscellaneous works, and Sundays theology. Thus I intend, by the help of the Master, to improve the golden moments as they pass." One would have thought a routine like that would keep golden moments down to a minimum.

During the period 1841–1843, he kept a copybook which reveals details he chose to omit from his autobiography. The copybook, which is owned by Professor Charles Thomas, portrays the emotions that stirred the developing poet. The opening sonnet is rueful and life-weary. Harris is suffering from a "sad and sorrowing complaint" which renders him pale of visage. He is subject to "weeping vigils" and contemplates his own extinction:

> *He bids farewell to life's delusive scene.*
> *For labour gripes; and ever-gnawing care*
> *Hurries me weeping onward to despair.*
> *Misfortune weaves for me her painful lore,*
> *The grave devours me, and the struggle's o'er.*

John Harris's complaint was obligatory for a man of his years: he had fallen in love. The woman, Professor Thomas maintains, was Eliza Thomas (1814–1847), some six years older than Harris. She lived at Treslothan with her widowed mother and two sisters, Susanna (1810–1881), who became a bookseller of Basset Road, Camborne, and Sophia (1806–1855), who married John Bartle of Stithians, Truro. All three sisters wrote poetry and formed a small literary coterie which included their cousins, Charles and John, George Bull and his wife Gertrude, and the daughters of John Budge, the well-respected Quaker. Visiting them was an aerating experience for Harris, who had been hitherto starved of culture. He would call upon the Thomas sisters and talk of poetry, literature and religion. It was at "the lovely home of the Misses Thomas," he recalled, "that I first heard Mr. Bull read some choice extracts from Byron's *Childe Harold.*"

The home which Harris visited with an accelerating heartbeat was a long thatched cottage situated along the footpath running through the hamlet of Treslothan to Silver Well Lane, which links Stennack with Lower Carwynnen. The Thomas sisters had more money than Harris and were perhaps better connected. Their father, William Thomas (born 1761), had been a Bolenowe farmer who had married their mother, Mary, in his forties. He died in 1832 and left them ten acres at Treslothan as well as a share of family land at Bolenowe.

A rather dashing analogy* has been made between the three sisters and Louisa May Alcott's *Little Women*: Sophia the eldest resembled Meg; the adventurous Susanna (who went travelling in France in 1843) is like the literary Jo; pensive, ailing Eliza recalls Beth. All three had literary inclinations. Acrostical poems in the copybook are set beside domestic elegies such as the lines by Susanna on the death of her cat. Susanna's animal bore an original name: "Beside the margin of a lofty wood, an humble cottage stood, and there poor Tasso died."

Having private means and wit enough to name a pet after an Italian court poet of the sixteenth century, the sisters must have delighted Harris, who was not used to animated discourses, even without the added attraction of cultivated female minds. Meeting the sisters intensified his awakening need for love and empathy – for a helpmate to provide emotional relief from his life of isolated effort. His relationship with Eliza was platonic yet he desired communion of a closer sort. But his tentative advances received no encouragement. In a poem dated November 1842, he pondered gloomily on the passage of the seasons, ending with *lines addressed to his mistress*, winter:

> *When Cold's rough finger chilled the blood*
> *And Life, and Death, hard panting stood,*
> *When Hope, and Fancy, both were tired*
> *And Love herself had just expir'd*
> *T'was then I felt a flame for thee:*
> *And canst thou feel the same for me?*

The last lines were directed at Eliza. Does she return his love? Unfortunately it seems that his wintry mood was an apt one. Eliza may have turned down a proposal of marriage: the copybook

*See *Poetry at Treslothan* by Charles Thomas.

contains another poem entitled *Lines Written After A Keen Disappointment*. It begins dejectedly:

> *T'is now the dead of night,*
> *And I sit down to weep . . .*

Subsequent details of the story have been filled in by Professor Thomas in his monograph. Eliza Thomas married a young man, Henry Stephens of Penventon, Treslothan, but died shortly afterwards, aged 32, probably of consumption. She was buried in May 1847 in Treslothan churchyard where Harris's own beloved daughter, Lucretia, is laid.

Harris was deeply affected by her death. Not long after, he wrote *Treslothan*, a poem in which he recalled his lost friend:

> *Ay, one there was more beautiful than all,*
> *Which lingers with me as a glittering gem*
> *Amid the shadowy vistas of the past,*
> *The happy home of poetry and love!*
> *Alas! how changed! The voice of song has ceased,*
> *And hearts unstirred by music slumber there . . .*
> *The hand is frozen with the frost of death,*
> *In the damp grave beneath the aged tree.*
> *Peace to thy shade, Eliza! Slumber on,*
> *Where noise and riots never dare intrude.*
> *The sigh that rends the heart-strings, and the sob*
> *Riving the walls of the clay tenement,*
> *And shaking furiously life's prison house,*
> *Will rack thy peaceful bosom no more.*
> *Peace to thee, gentle sleeper! May the friends*
> *That planted o'er thy head the early rose, –*
> *So emblematic of the Muse's child, –*
> *And he who drops at eventide the tear,*
> *Rejoin thee in the skies! O, when I think*
> *Thy spirit is in heaven clad in white robes,*
> *And o'er the flowery banks of Paradise*
> *Gliding with angel bands, hymning his praise*
> *Who bought thee with His blood, methinks I feel*
> *Increased desire to do my Maker's will,*

That, when I die, we both may meet again
In sweet companionship, – to part no more.

There exists a Thomas family copybook, containing some of the writings of the sisters. What emerges is that Eliza seemed to have an intimation of her early end. When only sixteen, she wrote about a friend "Edwin", who may have trifled with her affections, musing on how he would react to her death:

Will Edwin then think of my name with respect,
Or shed the warm tear on my tomb?
Will he visit the place where my body is laid
Or, when evening's soft bloom shall appear,
Will he think on the vows he so often has paid,
And bestow on my memory a tear?

This can be interpreted as girlish melodrama, but it may well have been rooted in the knowledge that her life would be shadowed by poor health. In 1838, when she was twenty-three, she wrote a poem, *Treslothan Cottage*, which is as carefully crafted as anything in the Harris canon:

Sweet cottage, lowly as thou art
Inelegant of form,
Thy roof of straw, thy walls of stone
By skilless hands together thrown
Thou still hast power to charm.

The poem describes how the cottage was whitewashed and provided with a garden. Plants and flowers are happily itemised and then the mood darkens:

Retired from sorrow, toils and pain,
To thee Eliza death is gain.
Thy griefs are past, thy course is run
And brightly sets thy evening sun.
Attend Eliza's soft repose
With lilies' bloom and blushing rose.

Let none disturb her sweet repose;
She ne'er occasioned others' woes.

The above first four lines make the epitaph on her headstone at Treslothan where she is buried near her sister, Sophia. The verses can be read as purely derivative or as hinting at an Ophelia-like sensibility. Eliza had studied Shakespeare and the Romantic poets. All the life-weary exhalations are there: the listless attitudinising, the inevitable roses and lilies, the portrayal of death as a bitter balm. Such reading matter possibly reinforced Eliza's sense of physical frailty and it is sad to think that she only enjoyed six months of married life:

Eliza's death that year may have unsettled Harris, perhaps rendered him receptive to the supernatural, though it could hardly explain the incident at midnight, when he had just finished his shift at Dolcoath. Exhausted, he climbed up to the surface. Along with his fellow workers, he tramped down the path to the small blacksmith's shop where his day-clothes were hanging from iron pins. As he entered the shop, he heard a loud noise outside. He ran to the door and saw "a little horseman on a night-black nag, galloping furiously in front of the smithy . . . Round and round, and round the shed it rushed, at a frantic pace, each time faster, as if the weird animal had wings." Harris saw no whip or bridal reins in the rider's hands – nor any saddle-stirrup or spur. He was amazed when he saw the horse gallop away and scale a steep flight of steps which ran up the side of Bottom Hill. The animal "leaped from level to level, and from stone to stone, and it seemed at times that the black horse was standing upright on its hind legs."

Harris and his companions set off home, using the same route, believing that they had seen the last of the mysterious rider. At the last step of the footpath, before they reached the road, they were confronted by the spectral figure again: – "He seemed black as ink, armless and legless, and no bigger than a farmer's watchdog." Harris shouted to him "Good night!" but there was no reply. The black horse galloped away towards Tuckingmill, and they heard its ringing hooves fade into silence.

Less credulous was his response to a colleague who told him that an old man in the neighbourhood was a wizard, capable of laying any restless spirits who happened to be hovering in the graveyard. What aggravated Harris most about this elderly necromancer was that he claimed to be a man of religion. To effectively deceive the local folk, he attended chapel services, sang lustily and prayed devoutly. Harris visited the cottage of the alleged healer and found inside the father of a girl who had been unable to walk until the wizard had cured her in the name of God. This man had implicit faith in the "healer" and thought him almost omnipotent. When Harris censured the object of his adulation, he became angry and accused him of not believing the Bible. Harris replied that it was the old wizard he doubted and not the Holy Book. Whereupon the man said, "Say you so, say you so? Look at this trace of onions hanging against the wall. They belong to him, and if you touch them, and twist them about, you will have your head turned upon your shoulders."

Harris took up this unusual challenge. Making a dash towards the onions, he plucked them off the wall and throttled them. The father of the girl sank down, shattered and pallid, while Harris announced, "I have defied the enchanter on his own ground, and you see no harm is come of it. None but God can do as you say. Renounce your belief in such vile impositions, and trust in a good Providence, for He has said that the very hairs of our head are all numbered."

The father of the girl was still not convinced. "You have escaped for the present and only for the present," he roared at Harris. "On your way home, an awful catastrophe will overtake you. You are sure to have your head turned upon your shoulders, so as to be looking backwards." Feeling that he'd heard enough, Harris wished the man goodbye and made his way back. He reached his father's home at twilight, his neck still orientated in the conventional direction.

Chapter Six

Marriage

Solitary yet piously sociable, effusive yet taciturn, what image did Harris present to the opposite sex? Photographs show that he had an agreeable appearance, yet he records a story of how he was walking on Tregoning Hill and entered a cottage to ask for a drink of water. In the kitchen was a bent old crone with whom he conversed pleasantly for some time. She squinted at him through metal spectacles and enquired his age. He asked her to guess; she put him to be around fifty. Harris "ruminated on his antique appearance" as he walked home. He was only twenty-seven but miners often showed signs of premature ageing – sallow complexions, hollow eyes, sunken cheeks and stooping gaits. Only one in nine reached the age of seventy and 28% died before their thirtieth birthdays.*

Her miscalculation did not cause him to despair, for by then he had already acquired a wife, not long after his proposal had been turned down by Eliza Thomas. In 1845 he had married Jane Rule of Troon, the daughter of a miner and smallholder. "I became the proud possessor of my good wife Jane," he stated. An unfortunate choice of phrasing from a feminist standpoint – his views were not that radical.

Harris may well have made up his mind to marry even before he had ascertained the identity of the fortunate young lady. Earlier on, assisted by his brother Will (who emigrated to America in May 1845), he had cut out blocks of granite from Bolenowe Carn in preparation for building a house. Whether he had a future wife in

*From statistics released in 1871.

mind, one does not know, but he was a prudent man, aware of a certain inevitability in the tide of human affairs.

In his autobiography he wrote, "Love meets him on his flowery pathway and he weaves a chaplet of choicest roses to adorn her head. He worships at the shrine of beauty till they stand before the sacred altar and the two are made one." It is easy to grow impatient with such sentimental blancmange. His early works are full of sighs, kisses and painful longings, since, understandably, he wished to elevate his personal feelings. We must assume, however, that the poet who intuitively responded to Burns knew all about the blunt basics of existence.

Despite his religious fervour and desire to better himself, Harris was not stiff and severe. Beneath a crust of solitary reserve, he was a genial man who lived much of his life in a state of suppressed excitation. And what made him particularly happy was the company of women. Even as an elderly writer, he was eloquent in his praise of romantic love, weddings and all the paraphernalia of affection. As a young man, he was passionate and attentive to the opposite sex – the love scenes in his poetry hint at this. Young women allowed him to unfold his inner self. For instance, he wrote lines to an admirer who sent him a laurel wreath – a type of flattery a poet could not resist. He was not a man's man, the type who would attend a club and exchange backslapping banter, but a Romantic spirit who wished to wring beauty and poetry out of everything. Instinctively he felt that women would value this attitude more highly than men (although it was actually a cool-headed Methodist business man who raised the cash and got his books published).

Another aspect of his poetic side was a total lack of aggression. In his *Autobiography*, not one unkind word or remark is passed about anybody. There is no settling of scores or personal raillery. John Harris was incapable of that sort of thing, and if his seriousness and piety sometimes intrude, it is necessary to remember that humour needs moments of relaxation and spontaneity of which Harris had few in his arduous life, and his humour does not rely on wit, satire and sarcasm, but delights in comical intimacies and domestic mishaps.

When Jane Rule got to know John Harris, she was becoming acquainted with an unusually receptive and intelligent man. A preacher and poet who spurned coarse language and valued flowers and the Cornish countryside above taverns and tobacco, he must have appeared to her as someone out of the ordinary – even a Prince Charming with his gift of language. And despite the testimony of the lonely crone of Tregoning Hill, he had an open, friendly face, which women may well have found attractive.

Details of courtship or engagement are not available. But reading between the lines of the poems, it is possible to make certain speculations. Obviously, then as now, getting entangled in a relationship had its drawbacks. Hard-pressed miners had little time for dalliance and there was also the question of privacy. Where could young couples in remote country districts go to be alone? The cottages tended to be smoky and crowded with parents, siblings and animals; to enjoy moments of intimacy, many had to endure the rainy outdoors or wait until the warmer months. Courting couples of Troon lingered in the primrose-studded lands or more adventurously climbed the high, heathery slopes of Carn Brea. There were rocky nooks where they could embrace without embarrassing or startling anyone save the wild goats. In the autobiographical *Monro*, Harris states:

> *Thus passed his teens, thus passed his riper years,*
> *Until Love met him on the April plains,*
> *Where she sat sighing in a shower of tears,*
> *While primrose-clusters whispered in the lanes,*
> *And gentle songsters chimed their sweet refrains*
> *By old farm-gate on budding bush and fence.*
> *His love, perhaps, was like all other swains,*
> *Although, I ween, a little more intense.*
> *Holy, unselfish, deep, angelic-like, immense.*

So John Harris drew closer to Jane Rule when the weather was getting warmer and more conducive to romance. Although James Howard Harris described Jane as the daughter of a "neighbouring farmer", the Rules were as much a mining family as the Harrises. They must have owned a farm or smallholding which provided them with some kind of independent income. It was alleged locally that, "as baby boy and infant girl, the couple had been baptised in the same water . . ." Jane had lost her young mother, also Jane, whose maiden name was Penpraze, when she was a mere child. She had died at the age of 26, leaving her husband, James, to bring up the children. In 1827, James Rule remarried and produced five sons and three daughters.

The stepchildren made for a lively household, but they were all very much younger than Jane, who may well have had to do a lot of nursemaiding. Seven years later, in 1834, her younger brother, Frank Rule, died, and by then she was probably feeling miserable and exposed. She left her crowded home for a period before her marriage – her name does not appear on the 1841 census – and, when Harris got to know her, she was working as a milliner. She was the same age as Harris and also in need of a domestic anchorage; he may have been able to offer her the affection and comfort her home lacked.

Harris described how his feelings resembled those of other bucolic lovers, "though, I ween, a little more intense." But why was Love "sighing in a shower of tears" – what was upsetting her? Is a personal allusion hiding behind this – for artists do strive to achieve a kind of honesty about the events that shape them. Had Jane suffered a personal hurt of any sort? Or is Harris employing a conventional conceit: Love alone and wistfully awaiting a partner? Or is this being unduly portentous over an obvious rhyme for "years"?

If Jane, like other girls, helped on her father's farm, it seems likely that Harris made approaches to her in that setting. Despite his mastery of words, his courtship was shy, full of hesitant ploys, bashful lingerings and snatched conversations. Not everything he wrote in *Carn Brea* is by any means autobiography, but this passage, dealing with the wooing of Laura, has a delicate exactitude:

> *When she walked*
> *In gentle girlhood through the peat-hedged meads,*
> *To milk the cows beneath the flowery thorn,*
> *He whistled at the gate, and saw her home.*
> *And if at eve she took her waterpots,*
> *To fill them at the fountain, there was he,*
> *Conversing by her side, and aiding her*
> *To cross the narrow stiles with granite steps,*

Bearing the pitcher even to the door.
And when she rode from market, holding fast
The basket on the lap, he strove to steal
Across the lane, with business on his brow,
Or true or false, he cared not, so he caught
A smile from her to gladden all his care.

The wedding took place on September 11th 1845 at Camborne parish church. It appears to have been a muted affair, sadly devoid of merriment:

No church-bells rang upon his wedding-day,
  No white-robed bridesmaids by the altar stand,
No village gossips throng the public way,
  No branches wave, no lifting of the hand;
But quiet as a footfall on the sand.
  Two aged sires were all that gathered there,
The loving fathers of a different band,
  Called hence long since to breathe a purer air,
Where Heaven uplifts her towers and all is passing fair.
(Monro)

There is no account of his mother at the ceremony. He remembered her watching him leave the home door with tears in her eyes, "for she was parting with her loved first-born." Like Shelley, Harris was drawn to the colour white, symbolising purity and spiritual illumination. White rocks, white robes, white daisies, white clouds – usually he overflows with chaste imagery but here draws attention to the absence of "white-robed bridesmaids" by the altar. Was there an element of haste which made the union imperative?

It seems likely that Jane was over two months pregnant on the day of her wedding. While this placed added pressure on Harris and may have set a few malicious tongues wagging, it was not a subject of scandal and concern. Being a local preacher, more was expected of him than the average man, yet in country districts pregnancy often preceded marriage, even among the devout; the emphasis was on the child being born in wedlock rather than conceived in it.

For this most important day, the young Methodist preacher chose a minimum of ritual. Neither were there friends or guests. Is discretion evident in the small congregation? Probably not; working-time was precious among the poorly paid and it was common for marriages to be witnessed by just the sexton and a relative or two. The fathers – John Harris Senior and James Rule – were logical choices.

And what of his new-found bride? What can be said of Jane Rule? Clearly she was loving and diligent as any wife of a thoroughgoing Methodist, but it seems certain that John Harris was the more assertive of the two, the patriarch of the family. I assume this because many women might have frowned upon – even actively opposed – his obsession with producing poetry when making an honest crust was a formidable problem.

Obviously there was a deep empathy. Harris makes it clear that Jane shared and understood his desire to gain distinction as a man of letters. But the number of references to her in his auto-biography, compared with those granted to other relatives and associates – or even Old Golly the horse – are remarkably few. This suggests that Jane, while appreciating her husband's special gifts, had a self-effacing disposition, for Harris was a comparitively respected local personage, and as his spouse one could do little but support and admire. In the poem *My Little Wife and I*, Jane is praised as "the daintiest flower" and "a faithful critic" of his "rhyme-scraps" and there are some touching tributes to her in his later writings.

Following marriage, his next priority was to find suitable accommodation for himself and Jane. They first set up home together in a two-roomed dwelling in Troon overlooking the scars and refuse of Polgine Mine:

> *Among the mine-pits was my second home,*
> *With earth's red ribs surrounded, hacked away*
> *By Cornish heroes underneath the sod,*
> *And piled in heaps on the disfigured plain.*

No doubt Jane's condition was good news, but it also increased the need for living space. Harris's skills as a tributer earned him no more than ten pence a day for the first ten months of their married life. He must have felt grimly conscious of the lowness of his income when a daughter, Jane, was born, April 1st 1846. And then he had some good luck. During the summer of 1846, he discovered a rich vein of ore, for which he was rewarded with the sum of £200. This enabled him to start work on the home he needed urgently for his wife and daughter.

The plot he selected was at the east end of the present Pendarves Street on the north side. Assisted by his father's horse, Old Golly, he carted stones from the quarry downhill to Troon. Evenings, mornings and sometimes by moonlight, too, he shifted the heavy granite blocks for two years, while other miners watched, smoking pipes or attending to their own allotments. Exploding a romantic myth is rather a low practice but there is some doubt as to whether he actually "built" the house with his hands. Most likely he employed a local mason, skilled in working with rough-hewn stone, for the walls, and a carpenter for the door, first floor and roof. This would have more plausibly accounted for the expenditure of £200. Although less than half a mile distant, the setting was more open and rural than his previous home and had a little stream running by which delighted the poet:

> *My third was 'mid the rushes by the rill,*
> *Babbling its beauty to the tall blue-bells,*
> *Which kiss'd its waters as they sparkled by.*
> *'Twas a small nest, with a pleasant garden-ground*
> *Built for myself.*

Harris moved into his new home in March 1848, having put down a capital sum on the plot twelve months previously; the first rent was paid the following spring to the Pendarves estate. The building was far more primitive than anything now occupying the site. Miners' "cabins" as they were called tended to be dank boulder-built thatched cottages with earth floors and windows put together out of fragments of bottle or bits of broken glass. There was no running water, no sanitation, no lighting save that provided by candles and rushlight, and no comfortable furniture – a bench, a hard wooden settle, a few stools and a bed of sacking stretched over a timber frame. Such a building, with only one or two rooms, might have to house the miner, his wife and a brood of five or six children. Furthermore there was the likelihood of unpleasant accidents such as children falling into the cess-pit or being savaged by the resident pig.

Harris's home at Troon Moor was more salubrious than Camborne town itself with its streets awash with slops and soapy water thrown off by washerwomen. "There is no proper sewerage in the place," observed the *West Briton*. "Many back entrances are excessively filthy and Gas Lane is the abode of filth, both physical and moral. There are causeways to nearly every line of houses, but so bad, either from want of being paved, or being so badly paved, that there is no pleasure in going over them. There is no flat pavement in the town . . . In the darkest winter there is no light except the occasional light that comes from the heavens, and the glimmering from the shop windows."

There is a picture of Harris relaxing, after a day of heaving stones, in the verse epistle *Home Thoughts From Abroad*, addressed to his brother, William, who emigrated to work the lead-mines of Wisconsin, only shortly after helping John cut stones for the Troon house. The style is a mixture of squalor and chocolate box but one gets a clear idea of the living conditions of the period.

> *Close shelter'd in my cot alone,*
> *Weary all day with carrying stone,*
> *To build my new home on the moor,*
> *So that my limbs are stiff and sore.*
> *Jane gone to market safe and well,*
> *And baby sleeps in slumber's cell;*
> *O see the poet's earliest flower*
> *Sweet-folded in her cradle-bower.*
> *The hens perch on their roost branch-high,*
> *The hog is grunting in the stye;*
> *Sod-thatched and nettle-cover'd, one*
> *I built myself since you have gone.*
> *It has a door, a grating door,*
> *Just eighteen inches high, or more,*
> *Through which poor piggy pokes his snout,*
> *Tossing too oft his bed about,*

To eat his turnips boil'd or fried,
And grunt for many things beside.

Despite the homely porcine talk, the ultimate fate of the animal
was to be dispatched by the local pig-killer, chopped up, cooked,
mixed with turnips and laid in a shroud of dough. Pasties were the
staple fare of Cornish miners. Soon after descending the pit, they
would remove them from their croust bags and eat them, to ensure
that the rats did not get there first.

Troon was not the stark suburb of Camborne one sees today.
Predominantly rural, it consisted of some thirteen two-roomed
buildings set in the vicinity of the present St John's Church and
accommodating some twenty-five families. Harris found its general
aspect agreeable and we get a glimpse of his domestic life in *Jane's
Epistle*, a letter-poem written in 1848, addressed to Uncle William,
now a miner in Wisconsin. One has to put on humid Victorian
spectacles to fully appreciate this bit of random rhyming written
for the little girl's second birthday. We learn that Uncle William
had sent her a "present of silver" – an American dollar? – and
that she has recently stayed at Six Chimneys with her grandmother,
who owns a grey cat with small feet. Father John has (inexpertly)
fashioned a manikin:

I've a short leaden Cupid, which father has made:
By the by, I don't think he has studied the trade;
For its eyes are projecting from out its rude head,
And its fingers and toes are like rents in a shed."

I've a smart-looking frock as the neighbours all said,
Which mother bought for me – a beautiful red.
I've a new pair of shoes, – O, I feel they'll be torn –
Brass-buckled brown-coloured, which yet are unworn.

I slept on the hill-top a fortnight ago,
But I'd much rather sleep in my cottage below.
Grandmother was kind; yet, though fondly caressed,
I would rather be home in my own little nest.

William Harris married the widow Agnes Jewell in 1853, who provided him with three sons and a daughter. When she died, around 1865, he married another widow, Jane Walters, 1st August 1866 in Dodgeville, Wisconsin. There was a frequent exchange of letters between him and John, who may well have drawn inspiration and factual data from the correspondence.

AMES HOGG, the Ettrick Shepherd, has somewhat humorously said, "I like to write about myself: in fact, there are few things which I like better; it is so delightful to call up old reminiscences."

Opening of John Harris's 'Autobiography'
– engraving by John Alfred Harris

Chapter Seven

Children

Harris's early years of marriage are a chronicle of unsparing effort. Money was constantly short, and if he worked a barren lode, he might have to apply for an advance or 'subsist' from the company:

> *He was a tributer; a man who work'd*
> *On speculation, digging through the ground*
> *In search of ore, the sweetener of his toil.*
> *If he found, he flourish'd, if not found, he fell;*
> *Nor fell alone, fell wife and family.*
> (Carn Brea)

Generally a tributer earned more than an unskilled miner owing to his greater experience and ability. He was employed on a contract basis, paying a "tribute" or portion of the value of the ore to the mine-owners.

As a poet, he continued to snatch precious moments out of the teeth of labour, using anything at hand to write on, from tea-wrappers to his thumbnails! A mild eccentricity began to take hold. He spent many hours brooding outdoors and, as the Cornish climate was erratic, cranial protection became an issue of some importance. He wore an old battered silk hat of which he was especially proud, for it had been made in Paris. It doubled as a paper-rest when inspiration descended. Sitting down in various rural nooks and hidey-holes, he would scribble down a verse or two, using the hard, flat crown as a support. Eventually the hat became decayed and had to be thrown out:

Poor weather-beaten silker, how slight thou lookest now,
From what thou wert seven years ago, when perched upon
  my brow!
Thy shagless top, and silkless rim, how piteous to behold!
And sides, that seem cruelly crushed together with the cold!

In peaceful bowers we oft have been, far from the busy town:
And many a thoughtless canzonet I've scribbled on thy crown.
I wore thee on my bridal day – that sunny day of days;
But Time hath cudgelled thee in ire, and knocked thee several
  ways.

Meanwhile there was an improvement in the working conditions at Dolcoath. Previously workers had emerged out of the bleak hillside into a shed where they were offered cold beer. By the year 1845, owing to the efforts of Lady Basset, daughter of Lord Dunstanville and owner of 32 out of the 186 shares in Dolcoath, miners on coming to the surface received half a pint of beef soup at the footway. A warm room was available offering heated water and baths supplied from a steam furnace, along with clothes-drying facilities.

An innovation was to appear on the technical front, too, when a man-engine was installed during 1854–5. Michael Loam invented this forerunner of the escalator after a competition was set up by the Royal Cornwall Polytechnic Society in 1841. It was a series of small moving platforms attached to rods, and at every stroke of the engine, the men were raised twelve feet; they could then step on another rod, and the action would be repeated. This was a boon to many miners, especially if the main shaft was not a crooked one. Unfortunately the Dolcoath man-engine only went down 240 out of the 362 fathoms, and on one occasion it broke, hurling twenty men – Harris included – headlong into the pit.

O Loam, of the ease
Thy genius procured them and joyful ride
On the rod, while others descend by their side.
(W. Francis)

On the domestic front, however, things were blossoming. Marriage brought John Harris the children who proved his most enduring source of happiness, kindling his inspiration and filling his heart with an atmosphere of quiet celebration:

> Then children came, like flowers, to gem his shed,
>   Filling his being with a fuller joy;
> In fragrant clusters round his hearth they spread,
>   Whose healing odours care could not destroy . . .
>
> His rhymes he wrote while they were on his knees,
>   Or in the cradle sleeping by his side;
> Walking abroad among the silent trees,
>   Or on the moses of the moorland wide . . .
> (Monro)

His children became his constant companions during the actual composition of his verses. "They were never happier than when with me," he wrote, "nor I than with them." When he was thoughtful, they would sense it, containing their exuberance and leaving him undisturbed. After the grinding toil of Dolcoath, Harris would feel his spirits rise at the thought of being greeted by his children. When the going was hard and he could barely afford bread enough to feed his family, he would fill his outside pockets with blackberries, so that when his children came out to greet him, he would always be able to offer them something. Years later, when his family had grown up, he was to recall the small gleeful faces peering out of the window and awaiting his return:

> When toiling in the darksome mine,
> As tired as tired could be,
> How has the glad thought cheered my soul,
> My children watch for me!
> And as I oped the garden gate,
> Which led into the lane,
> How danced my heart to see once more
> The faces at the pane.

Two little girls with gleaming eyes,
With soft and shining hair,
And sweetest prattle on their lips,
Were watching for me there.
One in the grave is sleeping now,
And one has crossed the main;
Yet still I see, where'er I be,
The faces at the pane.

Old age has bound me in its bands,
And o'er the solemn sea
I seem to hear mysterious sounds
From unknown lake and lea.
But through the cares that lie behind,
Along the murky plain,
I see as if but yesterday
The faces at the pane.
(The Faces at the Pane)

Many Victorians tried to convince themselves that the poor actually enjoyed squalor and severe hardship. Too lenient an attitude, they argued, merely encouraged sloth and slack morals. The land was full of lazy irresponsible paupers all too willing to beget "nests of brats" and cast them on the parish. Harris was well aware of this attitude. His own father had known penury and experienced – not necessarily at first hand – the brutality of bailiffs. Stories of the rough justice doled out to miners who fell in debt were common as can be deduced from this graphic sketch in *Carn Brea:*

Strange foot-falls echoed on the threshold-stone;
The door was rudely open'd; when at once
Two men rushed in, with wildness in their looks, –
The landlord and a towering officer,
Who, spite of tears, and sighs, and hunger-moans,
Took an inventory of their furniture –
Clock, dresser, table, settle, stools, and chairs,
Bed, bedding, clothes-press, pewter pans and plates,
Old faded pictures, jostled much by time,
The hour-glass, and the cage without the lark,

And other items, such as knives and spoons,
With numerous tin cans shining on the shelf, –
And, scowling on the good man, left the home.

A notable character in the poem is Prudence Worth, the good Christian woman who loans money to the hard-pressed miner. Quite probably, she was based upon a known benefactress of the period. Whether as a young and struggling miner, John Harris Senior ever resorted to such charity is not clear, for *Carn Brea* is a confusing mix of straight autobiography and local hearsay. What is clear is that throughout the hard times he had lived through he had been an upright and dependable parent, standards he had passed on to his son, who was also exemplary in this area, cherishing his two daughters to the point of idolatry.

Jane, the eldest, was born in 1846 and "crossed the main" to America some six years after her marriage in 1871. He delighted in her company and gentle ways and wrote the charming *On Jane Finding a Primrose in the Middle of February* and several other effective pieces, sentimental after the Victorian fashion, but also musical and tightly controlled.

Lucretia, his youngest daughter, was born in 1849 and evoked a strongly affectionate response in him. When she was only a week old, he took out his quill and celebrated her charms:

Thou camest like a bird of song to my poetic fold:
I welcome thee, my trembling flower, though only seven days old.

He loved her with an intensity made poignant by its very brevity. The little girl, picking flowers, accompanying him on walks, crawling on his knees while he composed verses, was the sun who warmed those days of ceaseless labour. Lucretia, sweet-natured and responsive, became her father's trusting pupil; for his part, feeling that he was learning the lesson of innocence over again, he watched her antics with delight. As D.M. Thomas observed, she and her sister "brought out the sprightly, lyrical, careless anima that he tended to suppress." Unfortunately those presences who bring the greatest happiness may also confer the deepest sorrow. This is certainly true of children, and the great tragedy of John Harris's life came when Lucretia died.

Chapter Eight

Publication

Following the birth of Lucretia, Harris felt a growing concern about his future. He was not a miner by vocation, only by environment and necessity. But the occupation worried him, for it put his family at risk. Injuries were inevitable and Harris knew that the longer he worked below ground, the less chance he had of retaining his soundness of mind and body. Furthermore the widows of miners who had died or been mortally injured working underground were seldom left with the money to feed and house them and their children. Often they were forced to tread the narrow way between charity and abject begging, while some of the younger women resorted to prostitution, a well-established trade in 19th century Redruth, although lacking any decadent refinements: an ill-lit room, a quantity of cheap gin, an undernourished female body on a grimy mattress might be the best a client could expect.

Such forebodings were confirmed in 1848 when Harris's father passed away, his death hastened by a fall at Dolcoath. He was buried among the poor of Camborne.

> *His grave is with the poor,*
> *The rude, unlettered clan . . .*
> (Death of My Father)

This was a grievous blow to his mother, Kitty, who found herself unable to maintain the property to the standard required in the lease. She was forced to abandon her home two years later, an incident which Harris described to his brother, William, in a poem.

If moving was a worry to Kitty, her daughter and sons seemed to have got a good deal of fun out of it:

> *One mounted the chairs on his head,*
> *And rattled away in his glee;*
> *And one with a post of the bed*
> *Was racing – right happy was he.*
> *Another took up the bird's cage,*
> *And trundled away like a ball;*
> *And sister conveyed the red mug*
> *And pictures that hung on the wall.*
>
> *The clock on the top of the stairs*
> *Look'd forth with a sorrowful face,*
> *Grew silent as silent could be,*
> *Unwilling to quit its old place.*
> *Puss flew from the desolate hearth,*
> *Though never accustom'd to rove;*
> *She has also found a new home*
> *With mother beside the old stove.*
> (The Deserted Home)

Harris shared his mother's anxiety during this traumatic period. He was also grateful for the solace provided by his own family. But there was a more crucial development which leavened the burden of underground toil: his poetic facility was gaining in depth and assurance and was beginning to stir local interest.

Recognition came to him as follows. He had just returned from a day's work in the mine, when a man stepped into the garden, enquiring gruffly, "Does the young Milton live here?"

The visitor was the Reverend G. Collins, a Methodist minister. He was asked in and invited to share an evening meal, which he did, eating the onions with a spoon and exclaiming, "I like these fried leeks." Eventually the clergyman broached the subject of John's poetry and asked to see his latest production. He was handed a grossly sentimental piece called *The Child's First Prayer*. "He quietly read it," Harris recorded, "and before he had finished, I could see the tears running down his face."

At times Harris obviously finds it difficult to resist adding writerly touches to his material. Did the Reverend Collins actually weep? Were the fumes of chopped onions hurting his eyes? Allowing that the record is accurate, perhaps he was deeply moved by the sight of a young miner, holding a poem in scarred and calloused hands and reciting with such eager tension. Everything was against him mastering so gentle and civilised an art: the gnawing pressure of work, a growing family, uncongenial surroundings. Yet he had crafted a poem as well as any man with the advantages of a classical education.

The house that the Reverend Collins entered was cramped and lacking running water. Harris's clothes were probably rough, patched and tattered and he would have spoken with a Troon accent. As for the fragrant stanzas extolling a child's piety, they were linguistic affectations, borrowed robes. What a square peg Harris must have seemed! Amid the poisoned slagheaps and industrial carnage, a Pierian spring had welled up in solitary splendour.

The Reverend Collins was aware of the poignancy of the situation. He detected in this miner a special intensity and eloquence. Here was a working man with true missionary zeal, a yearning to be appreciated and listened to by an educated audience. From this point, the poet's career gained momentum. Harris had another poem *First Primrose* published in a Wesleyan magazine. It was read by the local Methodist author, Doctor George Smith of Camborne, who invited Harris to call on him at his house in Trevu. During one of these visits, he told the doctor that he would like to make an attempt at publishing his poems. The other meditatively paced back and forth, then turning replied, "John, copy some of your best pieces, and I will submit them to my friends and see what they say about it."

Fortunately responses to the poems were prompt and enthusiastic. Doctor John Wesley Etheridge, Methodist minister, classical scholar and poet, appeared to enjoy their unabashed sentimentality. He singled out for special praise two domestic ditties – *The Love of Home* and *My Mother's Voice*. "Encourage the author," he advised, "and he will take his stand among the English poets."

Harris sets this down as if it all happened by magic. He was unaware of the forceful aspect of his character which inspired Dr. Smith to act so altruistically. Much has been made of Harris being an ordinary working man, but actually he was an extraordinary working man. He wanted to live as a free-standing poet, the equivalent of crying for the moon in the context of his background and circumstances. He combined an innocent pride with an element of tunnel-vision. Three people lived and struggled inside him: the vital and sensuous poet, the sometimes strident, impassioned preacher and the hard-rock miner who knew everything about blood, sweat, disease and death. This exciting fusion of traits made a deep impression on George Smith and fired him to undertake a long-term enterprise which was to cost him much time and effort.

George Smith (1800–68) was an influential man in the Methodist circuit. He may have been related to Harris, whose mother – Christian or "Kitty" Harris – was the daughter of William Smith, a farmer and tinner from Beacon in Troon parish. Son of a local carpenter, he had worked his way up, marrying in 1827 Elizabeth Bickford, daughter of the inventor of the miner's safety fuse. An astute business man, he made a fortune as proprietor of the Tuckingmill fuse factory, became chief magistrate for the district in July, 1859, and brought out a three-volume *History of Wesleyan Methodism*.

Prompt in assisting the poet, he wrote a prospectus, contacted the better-endowed of the neighbourhood and invited them to subscribe to a forthcoming collection of poems by a talented miner. The book *Lays from the Mine, Moor and Mountain* (1853) was well received by press and friends alike.

Another helpful spirit was Captain Charles Thomas (1794–1868), the managing agent of Dolcoath. A pillar of the Methodist community, Captain Thomas was a local preacher who lived simply at Killivose. His uncle was Captain Jimmy Thomas of Bolenowe who had been so generous in loaning books to the young poet.

A local saying goes "The Thomases made Dolcoath and Dolcoath made the Thomases." Captain Thomas's career bears out this apophthegm. From an early age, he had worked his way up, securing the job at Dolcoath in 1815 and later acting as a consultant on mining matters. In 1832, he urged that the mine should be explored at a deeper level; the result was that rich tin deposits were found, and by 1860 he was financially secure. Captain Thomas took a benevolent view of Harris's writings. He told the poet that he was so engrossed by his first collection that he stayed up all night reading it. He volunteered to help Harris by showing the book to a certain mining magnate who earned thousands a year. But he did not turn out to be as large-spirited as Captain Thomas. He flung the book down upon the account-house table, saying "Let him work on, let him work on!" He refused to subscribe to a single copy, a reaction that wounded Harris to tears.

Lays from the Mine, Moor and Mountain was a substantial achievement, considering the unpropitious conditions in which the bulk of it was written. The opening *Love of Home* introduces themes Harris was to repeat *ad infinitum*: mortality and sudden loss, the horror of war, lust for foreign places, nature's glory, man's folly and the emollient of Christ's teaching. The domestic virtues, as one might expect, are placed securely in the forefront:

> *Delicious Home! beside thy blazing hearth*
> *What griefs are softened, what bruises healed!*

Christian Heroism, though cluttered with pietistic set-pieces, has an unsurpassable evocation of Dolcoath. The new man-engine is saluted for its speed and utility and Camborne receives a tearful tribute. A commonplace jingle contains a chilling intimation of the future:

> *And when I saw Lucretia with tear drops in her eye,*
> *I thought, like little sister, she might soon grow sick and die.*

A curiosity is *Chanochet and Wetamoe* which is appended with quaint notes on the religious and sexual customs of the Red Indians – "The lover . . . lights his calumet, enters the cabin of his mistress, and gently presents it to her. If she extinguishes it, she admits his addresses; but if she suffers it to burn unnoticed, he retires with a disappointed and throbbing heart."

One might reasonably ask: why should a poor Cornish miner choose to write about Red Indians? Such anthropological gleanings provided a holiday from introspection and satisfied a taste to show off miscellaneous information. The way had already been prepared: the novels of James Fenimore Cooper had sold well in England and poets like Longfellow and William Cullen Bryant were acquiring a popular readership. Harris was abreast of the times: sentimental primitivism made a hit two years later with the *Song of Hiawatha*.

More ominously, *Lays from Mine, Moor and Mountain* contains the seed of mannerisms which Harris was to develop more fully in later volumes. For instance, there are lengthy verse-dialogues wherein simple statements are swaddled by pages of superfluous description. Characters adopt a pompous and high-minded tone; a great deal is said but little happens. This is a pity as he could write effectively within the naturalistic convention.

The year 1854 saw a new government formed under the high-handed and bluffly charismatic Lord Palmerston. In the summer and autumn the cholera fiend struck again, killing around forty thousand. The war between Russia and Turkey was still raging: fear of attack from Russia was prevalent throughout Europe and British colonies and possessions in India, Australia and China. This fear stirred the passing of a militia bill and the discussion of a foreigners' enlistment bill. All this reached a climax with the official declaration by Britain of war against Russia. A national fast was observed on April 26th in grim deference to the impending struggle which a French journal spoke of as "a sublime spectacle of a nation humbling itself before the Almighty after it had buckled on the armour for war."

But how far these events occupied John Harris, one cannot guess. Doubtless the wastage of funds on a foreign war distressed him, yet it was not uppermost in his mind. For he had achieved the goal of publication which inevitably brought prestige, increasing his confidence and sense of adventure. But on a domestic level things did not improve. The following year (1855) the thermometer fell to zero. A grim period ensued, a year of blighted crops, fatal sickness and martial ardour as the campaign against Russia intensified. Food prices rose to almost famine level; a severe spell of cold continued through to June. Ice-floes gathered in the bays around the coasts; on the frozen Thames huge floating masses were ground together on the tide to the damage of shipping. Great mortality resulted, the deaths being twenty thousand above average.

When the weather at last got warmer, Harris took one of his few excursions: during the harvest, he went by horse and cart to Kynance Cove along with half-a-dozen others. He does not say who accompanied him but he was conveyed by way of the Nine Maidens and Helston over wide moors and lanes smelling of honeysuckle, below skies "where swallows floated and twittering birds made pleasant melody, more delicious to me for having escaped for a brief season from the sulphur and strain of the mine."

They reached the Lizard and its strangely streaked rocks. Driving over a road paved with serpentine, they slid along as if on ice. The Cove was no less a marvel. "It seemed," he wrote, "like some fairy palace which the next sounding wave would sweep away. The music of the billows among the shining breakers, and the flight of sea-birds from peak to peak glittering in the sun, revealed to me a region of enchantment like that which comes in dreams . . ."

> *The sands that lie on this Elysian cove*
> *Are all ring-straked with painted serpentine:*
> *The hollow caves the waves have fretted out*
> *Are dashed with images of flowery hues;*
> *And on the rocks, like beautiful psalm-leaves,*
> *Are odes of music lovely as the light . . .*
> (Kynance Cove)

This must have seemed on reflection like a brief interlude in paradise. But the streaming radiance held auguries – baneful shadows cast into the future. For heavy rains came in October, hard frosts and dense fogs in November and December. There were many storms and hundreds of ships were lost or wrecked in the biting north-easterlies. Then, towards Christmas-tide, when the British army were freezing in the trenches of Sebastopol, Lucretia was taken with pneumonia and died, aged six years and five months.

> *And art thou gone so soon?*
> *And is thy loving, gentle spirit fled?*

> *Ah! is my fair, my passing beautiful,*
> *My loved Lucretia number'd with the dead?*
> > *Ah! art thou gone so soon?*

She was buried in Treslothan churchyard, where Eliza Thomas had been buried eight years earlier, and where John Harris lies today. The poet had never before experienced greater sorrow. Depleted with grief, Harris brooded over the spot and imagined the times he had walked with Lucretia who stopped and played by an old sloe-tree.

> *But ere the white buds came again,*
> *Ay, ere the leaves were shed,*
> *The gates of heaven let in his child,*
> *His little maid was dead . . .*

Again he lamented her in *Once More Among the Brakes:*

> *My child, my loving one,*
> *Too quickly passed away . . .*

And yet again in *The Lonely Muser*, where he sees himself as a pensive man "gazing away in empty space" after the "dark-cloaked Reaper has just passed" and claimed his favourite:

> *And now among the reed he sits,*
> *That creek and common fills,*
> *Gazing away among the stars*
> *That gem the heavenly hills,*
> *And deems he sees his angel one*
> *Beside the Eden rills.*

Finally there is the poem entitled *Lucretia's Grave:*

> *'Tis where the tree-tops wave,*
> *And gleam with glory 'neath the summer sun,*
> *And gentle breathings steal among the boughs*
> > *When busy day is done.*

The feverish succession of poems testifies to the keenness of his grief. The first half of the 1850's had placed a severe strain on Harris. They were years when he savoured life to the full, yet there was the added responsibility of keeping the family fed and clothed. Also they were years of domestic happiness, cruelly disrupted by family tragedy. For Lucretia was not the only bereavement he suffered. In 1854, when the country was bracing itself for war against Russia, his younger brother James emigrated to work the gold mines of Victoria. Taken ill with dysentry during the voyage, he died at Melbourne:

> On the ocean-journey affliction came,
> And disease fasten'd on his frame.
> Thus he landed 'neath Australia's sky,
> To breathe a fervent prayer and die.

(The Death of My Brother)

* * *

Back at Camborne, exorcising his sense of loss through his poetry, his reputation continued to grow. He became a byword in the district, a working man of high principles and lowly birth, who urged his fellows away from the tavern and into the chapel. The middle classes approved because he flattered and condoned their values. He was gifted yet modest, no overreacher, but one who quietly sought to perfect his talents, inevitably an oddity among the country folk. Some thought that he had ideas above his station and disapproved of his literacy and learning.

One elderly matron, seeing him sitting in his shirtsleeves reading a copy of Burns, chided, "You ought to be ashamed of yourself! You, a local preacher and reading Burns!" For people in remote country districts, the lustier verses of the ploughman poet were the nearest thing to offensive or shocking reading matter. Judging from Spencer Ashbee's *Bibliography of Prohibited Books* (1877), there was a rich crop of Victorian pornography even before ventures like *The Pearl* (1879) and the emergence of men like Leonard Smithers. But apart from the private collections, few of these filtered westwards to the Duchy: hence those desiring erotic distraction might find the lines of Burns their sole alternative to a pure life. The Scottish poet was looked upon as an "atheistical socialist" and a sub-literature of his "dirty poems" printed as chapbooks used to circulate. That wholesome periodical *The Ladies' Edinburgh Magazine* (April 1876) compared Harris and Burns, adding that the miner's muse "has not been a Will-o-the-Wisp, a dangerous light leading to mischief and darkness, but a steady home-beam, a guiding star". Probably Burns also regarded his poetry as a "guiding-star", for it led him into the arms of numerous women.

When Harris's first volume went through a second edition, his fame spread further. A Mr. Henry Gill of Tiverton sent him a pound, enabling him and his wife to visit Land's End. Except for the trip to the Lizard, Harris had barely travelled beyond Camborne-Redruth before, and the sight of the westernmost promontory, with its churning surf and wild array of crags, filled him with excitement. He wrote to his friend Edward Bastin, August 28th, 1856:

The Land's End is the most sublime thing I have yet seen in nature. How the dark waves dash against those rocks, and foam and hiss, moaning hoarse tales of storms and shipwrecks, and callous wreckers in days of old. Everlastingly they come and go, smiting the walls of the old cliff with giant fury, and then recoiling in jets of foam! The lighthouse in the midst of the waters, and the sea-birds on the ledges of the rocks, or floating over the waves, or chiming to the hoarse bass of the billows, as they dash through the sparry grottoes – all endear it to the memory.

After surveying all this spume and tumult, Harris and his wife were taken back over the moor by the guide to their guest-house, and for the first time in their lives they spent a night away from home. He did not sleep well and speculated whether his "little white chamber" was full of elves who prided themselves on keeping him awake. But the following morning, he got up early and was able to appreciate the promontory. He saw the "light-house shining like an angel" and the immense vista of blue stretching out to the Scilly Isles. "I stood upon the crags," he wrote, "and recited Charles Wesley's hymn, and felt I had begun a new era in my existence."

Chapter Nine

Deliverance – The move to Falmouth

In 1857, the year of the Indian Mutiny, John Harris's first son was born, James* Howard Harris, who grew up to become a school-teacher at Porthleven and biographer of his father. But the miracle of birth did nothing to solve the poet's problems. He was approaching thirty-seven and had only twice been away from home. At Land's End he had glimpsed new frontiers; temporarily escaping from the dungeon of Dolcoath, feeling the wind on his face and tasting the spray. He longed for the expansion of his personality beyond the mine and sighed for pure air and "the inspiration of Nature and man." He needed a vocation "where I might sometimes see the blue sky, the fields and flowers, and hear the wild birds and rushing rivers."

Although he was by no means an old man, his health was impaired. Many miners by the age of thirty were physical wrecks, and by right, as D.M. Thomas observed, "Harris ought to have followed the normal course: toil, procreation and silicosis; followed by an early death." However, if not a resolute optimist, Harris did have unshakeable faith in the Gospel. Whatever was God's will would prevail. "If the mine must be my grave," he wrote, "so let it be; or if taken out of it, it was well."

Fortunately salvation came promptly. There was a knock upon the door of his Troon home. Harris let through two visitors; one was his good friend, Mr Edward Bastin, a local chemist, who had walked three miles through the twilight to inform him that the post of Scripture Reader was vacant at Falmouth. He urged Harris to

*He called himself John Howard in the biography of his father.

apply and said that he would use his influence to ensure that he got the job. At last, "as God would have it," the miner was delivered into the world of light and fresh air. Furthermore his new work was in tune with his convictions.

In the autumn of 1857, he moved to the port, first to 7 Wellington Terrace, afterwards to 6 Killigrew Terrace, and then to 85 Killigrew Road, next door to the house which bears the commemorative plaque. The process of pulling up roots was painful. *Carn Brea* recalls leaving the Troon house he had worked upon and coming to Falmouth:

> *My own hands raised the stone*
> *From an adjoining quarry, and our croft*
> *Yielded me granite, which I split and brought.*
> *And I had thought to pass my life away*
> *In its seclusion . . .*
>
> *But, no; it must not be. One autumn morn*
> *We started up, and left it in the mist*
> *Which gathered thick between our eyes and it,*
> *And by the sea-shore with our babes we came.*

As an emblem of their former life, they took with them a cutting from the elder under which Harris's grandmother, Joan, used to milk her goats. Over the years it grew into a large tree. Harris would fondly observe it, recalling the windy slopes of Bolenowe Carn, as it waved in the light and the sparrows pecked its berries.

Falmouth was an important port, although it had lost its primacy to Southampton as the headquarters of the mail boats or "packets" to New York. With its combination of fishermen's hovels and neo-Grecian terraces, bathing beaches and public gardens, it was a sizeable town for Cornwall, where high and low life jostled together. There were soup kitchens, a workhouse, almshouses, a retired Sailors' Home and several other charitable institutions which ensured that a Bible-reader would be kept busy. Not a great deal is known about the Scripture Readers' Society, save that it was established at the same time as the Falmouth Town Mission (1852) and shared a joint governing body. There was some

63

practical liaising, for the Scripture Reader was responsible for the Town Mission Library. Directories of the period list certain details. In 1864, for instance, the Society's treasurers were Messrs. A.L. and H. Fox and the secretary Robert Coome and its stated purpose was "to extend the knowledge of the gospel, irrespective of peculiar tenets, by domiciliary visits." It is best to picture Harris as a travelling comforter, not dissimilar to the army Bible-reader, a dispenser of gentle moral correction and a bringer of good news.

There being no dearth of seafaring trade, prostitution was rife in the town, and a correspondent of *The West Briton* reported that, "from early noon till late, very late in the night, the pavements are paraded by bands of abandoned women of all ages and shades of disrespectablity, flashily attired in gilded jewellery and flaunting gaily-coloured ribbons, who elbow their way along and rudely thrust honest, respectable women into the street. The Bank – from the Custom-house to the bar – reverberates with their language, whilst their screams and hilarious merriment break the rest of peaceable citizens quietly slumbering in their beds."

The setting down of new roots heralded a change of society. Harris's Methodism was ecumenical. Old friends such as John Budge had been Quakers and he was well-disposed towards the Society of Friends. Though he did not agree with them in every respect – he was not averse to titles or a little light reading – he was devoted to peace and plainness of dress. Falmouth was a Quaker stronghold and, in the context of the reputation that preceded him, Harris met several members of the influential Christian fraternity. He visited Penjerrick, the country home of Robert Were Fox, the leading Quaker, where he drank tea poured from a silver teapot, "the ore being raised from Dolcoath mine, from which I had been so recently released." Penjerrick was a kind of sanctuary for the thinking man. Harris celebrated it in a sonnet, admiring its "limpid rills and crystal waterfalls" as if it were located somewhere in the Lake District. The Foxes were zealous in their support of charitable institutions. They drew into their circle people who had distinguished themselves artistically or intellectually: Wordsworth, Carlyle, the philosopher John Stuart Mill and Charles Kingsley could be numbered among their friends. A semi-tropical garden added an exotic touch to the congenial surroundings, and their Quakerism was not in the least daunting or reactionary. In 1864, Caroline Fox, daughter of Robert Were Fox, had travelled to Par to see Garibaldi*, the Italian hero, admiring his picturesque red shirt and general aspect of "spiritual beauty and moral dignity." Earlier, in 1847, she had entertained Harris's contemporary, the sculptor Neville Northy Burnard, "a great powerful, pugilistic-looking fellow of twenty nine . . ." Caroline Fox died in 1871, but the tradition of hospitality continued.

Robert Were Fox ran a firm of shipping agents in Falmouth. He was described in 1848 as a strikingly handsome man with "strongly-marked black eyebrows and beautifully carved profile." The inventor of the Deflector Dipping Needle, which resulted in a more reliable type of ship's compass, he wrote over sixty papers for scientific journals and with his brothers started the iron foundry at Perran, making machinery for the Cornish mining industry. He was president of the Falmouth Dispensary and Humane Society, which provided medical help and advice to the needy, and he also took a keen interest in the Falmouth Town Mission and served as an elder for the Society of Friends. Kindly and perpetually curious, he had a captivating manner and a way with children which elicited the respect and love of many. Harris valued his friendship and paid him a tribute on the occasion of his birthday, April 26th 1877:

> *A grass-tuft trembling in the sun,*
> *A lark's lay where the field streams run;*
> *A cottage-hymn when day is done.*
>
> *An old man by his garden-tree*
> *With God's own book upon his knee;*
> *A troop of children by the sea.*
> (Robert Were Fox)

Not long after settling in Falmouth, Harris produced his second volume of poems *Land's End, Kynance Cove, and other Poems*

*Harris celebrated his visit unmemorably: "Welcome HERO of the free! Albion spreads her arms to thee."

(1858). *Land's End* begins with graceful ease and assurance; the blank verse is full-sailed, suave and stately. There is a memorable sketch of an old tin-streamer and the artless child of nature who befriended him:

> *Thus lived the boy, the scion of the heath,*
> *A wanderer in this rocky wilderness;*
> *And there were breathings which he sweetly heard,*
> *At morn, and noon, and softened evening-time;*
> *Mysterious throbbings of the outer world*
> *To the young heart within.*

The boy resembles the poet. He has no external perception of the web of institutions and acquired attitudes which press down upon the individual and mould his life and outlook. Instead he lives in a kingdom of the mind, an emblematic land wherein the forces of good and evil battle it out. The delighted inner eye does not analyse or penetrate the hard surface of things, opting for the pits and peaks. Opening with the sunlit music of the billows, the first part of *Land's End* closes with the personal testament of Harris crushed and weeping over the loss of Lucretia and the frailty of being human:

> *My heart is wounded and it will not heal:*
> *I pray not that it should;*
> *The world is cruel; there's relief in tears;*
> *I pour them out upon the far Land's End.*

The second part has aspects of the adventure story, featuring a vividly described shipwreck:

> *The stout bark in the clutches of the gale*
> *Writhed like a living thing, and then the winds*
> *Twitch'd her in pieces with their maniac rage,*
> *And hurled the fragments howling on the rocks*
> *Or drove them shivering high upon the heath.*

Kynance Cove is another triumph, evoking parts of *The Tempest* with its dream-palace imagery and unstrained fluency. It has gloomy elements, mingling joys with drownings, but the language achieves a pure mineral glitter:

> White castles, towers, and palaces uprise
> Built with chaste light, and roof'd with burning gems.

The following year *The Origin of the Species* came out, a scientific treatise setting forth the idea of man's ape origins. Its ripple spread to faraway Cornwall and Richard Gill, the son of Harris's close friend, John Gill, actually drew Darwin's attention to an error he had made. Harris probably classed *Origin* along with "books of the baser sort." As far as he was concerned, man was God-made, pre-ordained, rather than a fortuitous genetic combination. His own eloquently digressive tomes remained unswervingly devout:

> The truly wise obey their Maker's voice
> And love the Being that created them.

In 1860 Harris brought out *The Mountain Prophet, the Mine and other Poems*. One of the title pieces – *The Mine* – gives a graphic account of the discovery of copper and the processing techniques used during the early Victorian period. There is a description of an elderly dowser and a muleteer.

> Old Timmy was the driver of the mules,
> And he kept sixty shaggy skinny things,
> Fed upon grass and very little grain;
> And with his mules he visited the mine,
> A tramping troop, to carry off the ores
> In little bags upon their bony backs,
> Two upon each, up hill and down dale,
> To the sea-port where it was shipped away
> Across the waves, and fused to mineral slabs.
> (The Mine)

Old Timmy's mules are ousted by the coming of the railway. He turns them out on the common where they die during a fierce winter. The mine continues to prosper and is powerfully evoked:

> *All the air*
> *Was black with sulphur burning up the blood.*
> *A nameless mystery seemed to fill the void,*
> *And wings all pitchy black flapped among the flints,*
> *And eyes that saw not sparkled mid the spars.*

What is ironic, in view of Harris's poverty, is the uncritical way he depicts bankers and mineowners. He is curiously innocent in that he does not see them as sharks or exploiters, only as men who have been granted their due for working long and diligently. In *The Mine* he describes the estate of a rich man (a humble worker who struck lucky) in paradisial terms:

> *See'st thou that mansion on the woody slope,*
> *Where trees stoop down and kiss the river-waves,*
> *Or whisper on its marge; and graceful sails*
> *Glide up and down, and sea-birds float and dive?*
> *Along the shrubbery walk a lady comes*
> *Leading her children by the evergreens, –*
> *Two boys, with brows like bards and eyes like space;*
> *And one bright girl, with April on her cheeks.*
> *Grey deer are leaping round them, snowy swans*
> *Steer over silent lakes, and cooing doves*
> *Drop from tall trees to drink at glassy falls,*
> *Whilst in his noble dwelling Wealth sits down*
> *Dangling his shining keys with wagging sides.*
> *This hall is Henry's, his that lady fair,*
> *And his those children beautiful as morn.*
> *Now placed among the worshipped of the world.*

There is no hint of irony in that last line. Wealth in his pristine abode recalls God in Heaven. Rich men are like the kings of fairyland who dwell in ornate dream-palaces. Pacific and sweet-natured, the bright surface of things entranced Harris who believed in conscientiously ascending the ladder of ambition rather than storming the citadels of privilege.

That same year a fellow-rhymer with whom he had corresponded paid him a visit. Edward Capern (1819–94) was Devonshire's own postman-poet and like Harris had lived a hard life, working in a Barnstaple lace factory at the age of eight in order to support his sick mother and later delivering letters while composing poems. He had a strong singing voice which he used to broadcast his own melodies. He went on long walks with Harris, and they must have had a wonderful time, exchanging stanzas and compliments until the sun went down. Author of such forgotten gems as *Wayside Warbles* and *Sungleams and Shadows*, Capern's muse resembled Harris's with an added topping of clotted cream:

> *Soft are the winds that kiss the South*
> *And bright the sun that shines on high.*
> *A rich carnation is her mouth*
> *And blue as April bells her sky.*
> (My Love-Land)

And Harris celebrated his friend in unblushing cheerleader style:

> *God bless you, little happy things!*
> *How much from you we learn!*
> *So let us shout together here*
> *Our poet's name, CAPERN.*

The only photograph of Capern I have seen shows him as spade-bearded, glum and dyspeptic, but portraits of Victorian elders tend to look like that. Lord Palmerston had granted him £40 a year from the Civil List in 1855 – some of his poetry was fiercely patriotic during the Crimean War.

Initially the release from Dolcoath revived Harris's spirits. His new work enabled him to view his background from a fresh perspective. He had endured such hardship and suffering that his personal history took on the character of a revelation. God had plucked him from dark anonymity and given him position and respectability. And he was stirred by this irresistible compulsion to chronicle the tales of triumph and disaster, of piety, passion, poverty and pride, which his mother Kitty and others had related to him; and they should be placed in their correct setting, the pagan mountain of his childhood. The upshot was that, in 1863, Harris brought out the powerful *A Story of Carn Brea, Essays and Poems.* The title poem is considered by many to be Harris's supreme masterpiece. Its basic plot is simple enough: two horsemen, riding through a rain-storm, take shelter at the cottage of an elderly woman and exchange a series of stories, all of which are homiletic.

"Their tales," commented D.M. Thomas, "have a reflective piety and relished gloom appropriate to the atmosphere of rain and burial. In Chinese box fashion, intermingled with the poet's rapturous celebration of nature and God, the stories unfold; a sense of small country community, interrelated and concerned, surrounds and makes inroads into the poet's romantic solitude, just as the poor mining villages cluster round the primeval grandeur of Carn Brea."

Structurally *Carn Brea* is not an easy poem to grasp without re-reading. Voices break in on each other and it is not always clear who is speaking, the poet varying his personal testimony with the widow's story and the horsemen's speeches. We are treated to tales of conversion, drowning, starving, blindness and brutal accident. The melodramatic anecdotes are by turns harsh, sentimental, pious, violent and smoothly eloquent. The horsemen have been rather daringly likened to the severe and unapproachable "Angels" of Rainier Maria Rilke. In actual fact, they are rather a disappointment, like dramatic emissaries from another world who dispense orthodox pieties. Injected into the amorphous bulk of the poem are lightning flashes of power – of galvanic lyricism and eloquence. The fury of the storm is invoked (Harris is good on weather in all its moods) and the language jolts and plunges like the hooves of a galloping horse:

> But see, two riders and their foaming steeds
> Burst from the coppice like a thought of flame.
>   Through the mist
> Loom'd the great granite crags and castle-top
> Of mineral-marked Carn Brea, whose awful head
> Was drenched with rain, and pitted with the storm . . .
> Still onward dashed the horsemen. Bank and brier,
> And deep morass, and ditch with water drown'd,
> And lanes where ruts yawned hungry, and dark pits,
> And rivers wildly tumbling o'er their brims,
> And ruins green with age, or grey with years,
> And bogs with torture boiling, – all were passed,

> And in a cottage clinging to a rock,
> Where sat a lonely dame in linen weeds,
> They turned at last for shelter, while their steeds
> Smoked in an outhouse 'neath a roof of straw.

Passages of jarring awkwardness abruptly soar to heights of drunken religious joy. The world is sluiced with sunlight and all of nature is re-born:

> He walk'd along, delighted with the world,
> Delighted with himself, and all he met;
> His eyes beheld, in everything around,
> The Grandeur of the Highest. In the hills,
> Golden with heather, he discover'd God;
> In the rude rocks that ribb'd them, and the clouds
> That gather'd on their summits, and the light
> Which oped their revelation, clearly he
> Saw God; and in the valleys shining, God;
> In the dear wayside flowers, and narrow rills,
> The trees, and shrubs, mosses, and blades of grass,
> And humming bees, and sporting butterflies,
> And white sand-grains along the sea-shore, God;
> Above, below, and all around him, God.

Harris can be tense and terse as well as garrulous. Nothing can be straighter from the shoulder than this:

> My hero-miner is no gilt ideal,
> Pulled in to make a poem, but a man
> Who really lived, and acted, and expired . . .

There is a concise and focused directness about his description of an atheist:

> He wore an ancient hat, and shaggy coat,
> With buttons white as silver; on his shoes
> Were shining buckles, and where'er he went,
> His curly dog would bear him company.
> But on his face there was a settled gloom.

> He was a mighty reader, and devour'd
> Books by the parcel, books of the baser sort,
> Shadow'd with doubt, and doleful with despair.
> The Bible he believed not, never read
> Except to cavil; and the sun, and moon,
> And silver stars, green earth and sounding sea,
> Were on his calendar as imps of chance.
> He turn'd his forehead to the blushing sky,
> And with his lips he uttered blasphemies,
> And madly shouted, "There's no God, no God!"
> He vowed that heaven and hell were fables both
> And man would perish like the roving-kine;
> That all went down and rotted in the earth,
> And there it ended.

Gothic darkness vies with calm reflection and astounding realism such as the description of the blind violin player and his daughter:

> He wore a coat of bargain, and a hat
> Long mock'd by tempests and the pelting rain;
> A green eye-shade concealed his sightless orbs,
> And on his face the powder grains had left
> The impress of their riot, pits and ruts
> And fearful scars, with bottoms black and sides.
> One hand was splinter'd, half the fingers gone,
> And the dried wrist, all blacken'd with the blast,
> Seem'd like a moving cinder of charr'd wood,
> O what a wreck he look'd, a human wreck!
> And yet he sang and played so pleasantly,
> As if he were the happiest man alive.

Best of all, there are the personal moments when Harris intrudes into the narrative. We follow his footsteps up to the summit of the Carn and drink up the scents of summer:

> How often hast thou fed my early Muse,
> Crag-heap'd Carn Brea, when from my father's meads
> I scanned thy front, mist-clad or clear, deeming
> My mount and thee twin-sisters beautiful!

One bright May morn, when violets were rare,
I trick'd old Labour, and equipp'd myself
With poet's baggage, pencil, sheet and lyre,
And, walking o'er the moors, I turn'd my face
Towards its summit shining in the dawn,
As 'twere an old bard welcoming the young.
I cross'd the meadows, follow'd by our dog,
Who snuff'd the air and bark'd among the flowers,
Right happy to be free! The larks were up,
Singing among the cloudlets, and sweet song
Gush'd up from a hundred hollows. In the fields
The cottagers were busy with their spades.
And ploughs, and harrows; and perhaps they thought
I was a crazy fellow wandering weird.

The poem ends with a drowning fisherman whose scalp is pecked by a huge sea-bird. But as the horsemen leave the widow's cottage, they see a glow-worm in a rocky cleft whose shine is answered by the silvery blaze of a meteor: twin beacons of affirmation or God-light uniting tiny creatures and celestial things.

Harris took great pains to write in clear, standard English, purged of colloquialism or dialect. This is evident in *Carn Brea* but one can still detect beneath the surface the rougher music of a blunt, unaffected countryman, who relies upon native observation and pithy economies of phrasing as well as non-conformist rhetoric. This is why the poem is central to Harris's achievement, for it is rooted in the earth, in felt experience. Aside from the title poem, there are many lesser pieces in *Carn Brea*: fresh personal memories of a rural boyhood, poems of birthdays and bereavements, a vivid sketch of what it is like to be a Bible-reader and occasional verses such as the lines on the death of the Prince Consort. Albert, who died of typhoid fever in 1861, had a high sense of purpose which Harris admired:

But as he lived, so died he
Where Peace delights to bloom,
And now fair Art and Science
Embrace above his tomb.

Even more informative is the list of subscribers to this volume. They show an exciting social range, from noted literary philanthropists like the Earl of Verulam (from Verulamium of St Albans in Hertfordshire) to mining captains and fellow writers like William Catcott. Also there are local dignitaries, such as the former mayor of Falmouth, Robert Broad, notable peace campaigners, friends like Edward Bastin, Charles Thomas and George Smith. What, one asks, do they all have in common?

Trying to evoke Victorian Cornwall is like reaching back to a lost world, a world socially divided, not merely by class and money but by a sense of morality. Harris's contacts were not all Methodists; some were Quakers; some were Anglicans; some were ecumenical Christians, yet they shared a common sense of mission. Implicit in their outlook was the notion of spreading the Word and improving the common lot. This sense of mission formed a bond between people of widely differing income and status – a network of devout men and women. Victorian philanthropy operated by monied people-of-conscience sponsoring men like Harris, who propagated the good way of life and could move in both worlds while remaining essentially poor.

Chapter Ten

The Shakespeare Prize

With the publication of *Carn Brea* in 1863, Harris consolidated his reputation. Letters were sent, praising the moral strength of his writings, which, a lady wrote, were a bracing contrast to "the mysticism and imitation of Tennyson" affected by others. Some were almost ecstatic in tone. A certain Maria Fotherby wrote to him, assuring him that his verses would gain him a place in "that heavenly city – golden city shining far away – what fullness of spiritual communion, what perfection of intelligence will be there!"

Despite such fragments of adulation, making ends meet was difficult and there were also the problems created by his family. In February 1859, Jane had given birth to a second boy, John Alfred, who had a spinal defect which would render his career problematic. Later, he became a photographer and wood-engraver, illustrating several of his father's books, and there is a certain pathos in the naive, yet also effective, illustrations of plants and bucolic scenes found in *Walks with Wild Flowers* and subsequent volumes.

His fortunes, however, revived a little in 1863, when his friend Catcott, who called himself "the baker bard of Wells", sent him a clipping from a newspaper announcing a poetry competition to mark the tercentenary of Shakespeare's birth, April 23rd, 1864. It was organised by Coventry Town Council and the adjudicators were Lord Lyttleton, George Dawson and C. Bray, Esq. The prize was a gold watch for the winning poem. Harris was roused at the prospect. Shakespeare had always been his idol; he had pored over the plays and sonnets, finding many edifying saws and precepts.

Frequently he quoted the playwright to enliven his phraseology, and the thought of composing a poem was a challenge. It took him two evenings, writing it out beside the kitchen fire, and afterwards reciting it to his wife, who responded encouragingly. He posted the poem the next day and prepared for the three months wait after which the winner would be announced.

He was returning from one of his missionary visits to the poor of Falmouth, when his wife called down to him from the top of the stairs, "You have gained the prize – the gold watch." A telegram was there confirming that he had indeed won the prize and inviting him to attend the Coventry celebrations. But residing as he did in faraway Cornwall, with limited financial resources and a demanding job, he was unable to travel and participate, although he read a newspaper account of it.

Poetry and civic pomp are very different activities. One is private; the other corporate. One emphasises the personal; the other denies it, opting for grand attire and bland oration. That is why it is difficult to be ultra-serious about this particular peak in Harris's career. But such reservations are niggardly compared with the delight the poet felt at all the detail and preparation.

In Coventry the streets were hung with flags. Handbills were issued by the mayor, requesting the shops to close at five in the evening. The Corn Exchange was the headquarters of the celebrations and its orchestra was ornamented with crimson drapery and surmounted by a facsimile of the bust of Shakespeare over the poet's grave in Stratford Church. Wreaths, garlands, flags and flowering shrubs were arranged around the hall. The pillars were hung with scrolls, inscribed with the names of Shakespeare's plays, and over the orchestra was the appropriate motto:

> *Take him for all in all,*
> *We ne'er shall look upon his like again.*

The band of the Royal Scots Greys performed Nicolai's overture to *The Merry Wives of Windsor*. Attended by his sword and mace-bearers, the Mayor mounted the platform and opened the envelope, containing Harris's name along with that of the second prizewinner, who received a silver watch. The poem was read aloud to an enthusiastic audience, and the report added that "Mr

AN ODE

ON THE TERCENTENARY ANNIVERSARY OF

WILLIAM SHAKESPERE,

APRIL 23RD, 1864.

PRIZE  POEM.

OVER the earth a glow,
  Peak-point and plain below,
The red round sun sinks in the purple west;
  Lambs press their daisy bed,
  The lark drops overhead,
And sings the labourer, hastening home to rest.

The Shakespeare gold watch by John Alfred Harris

Harris is a Cornishman, whose book of poems, published some years ago, entitled *Lays from the Mine, the Moor and the Mountain*, received such encomiums from the leading literary journals as few poets have been favoured with."

A few days later the watch reached Harris accompanied by the note:

May 6th, 1864.

Dear Sir, I send you by tonight's post the gold watch awarded to you for your poem. The watch is manufactured by one of the first English firms, Messrs Rotherham, who have acted very liberally, and made it worth twenty instead of fifteen guineas, the amount which they will be paid for it. The watch presented to the Princess of Wales was manufactured by this firm who constantly employ upwards of two hundred hands in different branches of the watch trade. I hope it will be satisfactory to you.

The postman who delivered the prize was even more overjoyed than Harris. He danced around in the kitchen and shouted, "We have beaten them all! Hurrah! Hurrah! The barbarians of Cornwall are at the very top of the tree!" Neither would he leave until Harris had opened the parcel and shown him the prize, which turned out to be a very swagger timepiece. On the centre of the case was engraved a portrait of Shakespeare, and inside the case were the famous lines:

> *Tomorrow, and tomorrow, and tomorrow*
> *Creeps in this petty pace, from day to day,*
> *To the last syllable of recorded time.*

To the locals of Falmouth, the award confirmed that Harris was truly a poet in the zoological sense. After all, a group of educated gentlemen in a faraway city had given him a solid gold watch for his rhymes! The manuscript of the poem, framed and mounted, was sent to the Shakespeare museum at Stratford-on-Avon where a copy of it may still be seen upon request. The tercentenary poem, selected out of over a hundred entries from England and America, does not demonstrate Harris at its best. Skilful, disciplined and varied as it is, it fails to grasp the knotty, psychological core of

*Portrait of
John Harris
from
frontispiece
to
'Wayside
Pictures'*

*Portrait
John Alfred Harris*

*Portrait
James Howard Harris*

Jane Harris and her daughter, Jane

Falmouth
Engraving by G. Townsend, c. 1850s

Redruth Railway Station
Engraving by G. Townsend, c. 1850s

Kynance (Cove)

*Falmouth (docks), view over docks to railway station, c. 1865
– station opened in 1863
photo: J. F. Trull*

Six Chimneys (Harris's birthplace) today with outhouse to the left

Six Chimneys (Harris's birthplace) at Bolenowe. This outhouse probably incorporates parts of the original building which fell into ruins

Tincroft, Bal maidens and other surface workers – mine captains in white coats
photo: Bennetts of Camborne, c. 1890s

Camborne, Basset Road c. 1870. There is no face in the clock tower – this was installed in 1874. Clock tower built in 1866

Illogan, Carn Brea from Church Lane, Redruth
photo: J. Valentine, c. 1890s

Dolcoath, "The chief mining district of Cornwall"
photo: J. C. Bussow, 1892

Camborne, Bolenowe, view up hill 1897
Captain Jimmy Thomas's house on right. Behind, whitewashed thatched
cottage of John Stoneman, farmer

Shakespeare (an almost impossible task!). What it amounts to is a kind of extended paean of praise, enumerating the multi-facetedness of the bard. Harris places himself at the centre, the young Cornish poet "stretched upon the moss" whose "soul is hot with joy" after contemplating the works of "Great, glorious Shakespeare . . ." The dramatist's characters rise up before him in a pageant:

> He hears the tramp of steeds
> Sees war in gory weeds,
> Roams through the forest with delighted eyes;
> Bends to the tempest's roar,
> Weeps for the monarch poor,
> And sobs with sorrow when poor Juliet dies.

The "musing boy" or young John Harris is handed the lyre of inspiration by the "genius of the height" or the spirit of Shakespeare, and he in gratitude composes a hymn of praise to his benefactor:

> He sang of him, the great,
> Shakespeare, of kingly state,
> Who in his boyhood by the clear Avon strayed,
> Learning the lore of song
> From feeble thing and strong,
> The great tree towering and the tiny blade:

> He solved the human heart
> Like a mariner his chart,
> And passion's every phase was known to him;
> And when the full time came,
> Forth burst the mighty flame,
> To blaze and brighten till the stars are dim!

Chapter Eleven

Out of Cornwall – To Stratford and Malvern

Following the award of the gold watch, Harris made a pilgrimage to Stratford-upon-Avon. He had reached the age of 44 and had never been out of Cornwall before, so he was only too glad of the adventure. How he financed the journey is not clear. The winning of the Shakespeare Prize may have attracted new readers and sponsors but perhaps a good deal of the cost was met by his friend and fellow-traveller, William Hooper, who was in sympathy with his cultural and religious interests. Together they visited Bristol, Clifton, Hereford, Worcester, Gloucester, Malvern, Birmingham and Stratford upon Avon.

Travelling to such exotic places produced a spate of poems. At last Harris had an opportunity to extend his topographical range beyond the boundaries of his native county. He went to Bristol and met benefactors like George Muller, founder of the famous orphanages, and visited Chatterton's memorial in St Mary's Redcliffe. Touched by the story of the boy poet whose genius had been spurned by those who should have nurtured it, he speculated whether Chatterton's soul might have benefited from "Bible-light" to guide it away from the path of forgery and suicide:

> *Poor gifted boy, thy native place*
> *Had small regard for thee,*
> *Who in a garret's gloom drank up*
> *The draught of misery.*
> *And now they raise thy monument,*
> *In boy-weeds looking down,*

With mutely mournful sad rebuke,
On the great smoky town.

O Chatterton! O Chatterton!
How soon thy race was o'er.
Pale Pity by the monument
Weep tear-drops evermore.
I saw a little beggar-boy,
With his blue half-covered limb,
Under his Gothic pedestal,
And then I thought of him.

The climax of his travels came when he arrived at Stratford. He enthused over the Avon meadows, Ann Hathaway's cottage and Shakespeare's grave, praising them in wholly conventional rhymes. Harris was neither exercising his imagination nor his powers of observation, only a facility for quick versification. In fact, the most exciting comment elicited from the pilgrimage was one of mild anger. Entering the room where Shakespeare was born, he observed that "every inch of the walls and ceiling is covered with visitors' names", which he found very shameful, "when they can be as often inserted in the visitors' book."

Fragments can be salvaged from this journey which he was to recall with more eloquence and flair in his poetic autobiography *Monro*. Taking a rest after a long train ride, Harris and Hooper climbed Malvern Hill through a shroud of fog. The poet was impressed with the magnitude of the eminence – he thought the mounds of Cornwall "mole-hills" in comparison. At the base of the hill, he was mobbed by a host of donkey boys, each one excitably extolling the virtues of his steed:

Full suddenly, under the dark trees hid,
We came upon a troop of noisy boys
With patient donkeys saddled skilfully;
And dinning was their native eloquence
That we should hire them: "Take my donkey, Sir!
My donkey has been eating oats today:
A fine beast mine; he'll bear you to the top
Without a hoof-slip. Try my donkey, Sir!

That fellow's Neddy is so lean on straw,
He has nought else. Mine has the finest food.
How sleek his sides, and what an eye is his!
How glossy is his coat! Just stroke him down.
Look at his ears. Please take my donkey, Sir!"
And thus they piped away with voices high,
But long had we been journeying on by train
Drawn by the horse of iron, and were glad
To press our feet upon the earth once more.
(Malvern in the Mist)

The moralist in Harris is abandoned for the moment; and in its place there is a realistic vignette. The donkey boys have a life of their own, and their cheerful banter comes over authentically.

Nevertheless, though the journey did not yield fine poetry, Harris found out to what extent his reputation had become enhanced socially. While he was being shown around Bath Abbey, a lady said to an official, "This is John Harris, the Cornish poet." This failed to produce the minutest quirk of the eyebrows, but then she added, "This is John Harris, who won the Shakespeare prize," and the man took off his hat and bowed.

The man who had encouraged him to enter the Shakespeare competition, William Catcott, received a poem from Harris on the occasion of his birthday the following year, February 28th, 1865. The miner offers his fellow-poet a laurel crown:

The singer now
Gets scarce a leaflet for his brow.
No laurels cluster round his head,
But Sorrow's weeds are there outspread,
Bound by Neglect's cold fingers drear,
Upon the brow of bardie dear.

The appalling "bardie dear" is repeated throughout the eight verses. Catcott probably appreciated the tribute. His collection *Morning Musings* was enthusiastically alliterative in the Harris vein; the titles alone (*Cornish Violets, My Village Home, Drunken Ned, Daisy on my Mother's Grave*) reveal him as a connoisseur of the twinkling tear and soulful sigh. This might appear an irrelevant diversion, but understanding Catcott helps one place Harris more firmly in his context. For here was another poetical labourer who found himself pursuing an uncongenial role.

Born in West Horrington, near Wells, in 1808, Catcott was the son of a stocking-maker and part-time miner, while his mother seems to have been a pious woman with a good singing voice. As a young man, William was intelligent and sensitive and tried to better himself by seeking employment in London. But after pacing the pavements for nine days, he was glad to accept work in a baker's shop for thirteen shillings a week, plus bed and food. After nearly three years of such drudgery, he returned to Wells where he continued the trade penury had forced upon him. His life was "one long Sabbathless round of toil with wearisome nightwork" –

> Half the night, besides the day,
> Bakers toil for little pay . . .
>
> Mark their faces as they pass,
> Blanched with sulphur, heat and gas . . .
>
> From the oven's mouth they go,
> Through the rain and through the snow . . .
> (Morning Musings)

Like John Harris and Edward Capern, William Catcott was a kind-hearted, benevolent spirit. He would have favoured a job less menial, less unrelenting, but instead he sweated day and night producing loaves and breakfast rolls. The value of such a friend to John Harris can be imagined. Both were lovers of flowers and the countryside and both had strong religious tendencies. On the several occasions when they met, they were able to ease each other's sense of frustration and suffered injustice by lending a sympathetic ear. Working-class poets today are still regarded as oddities. How much more sharp their sense of isolation in Victoria's day when literature was often the preserve of the rich and educated.

Twelve years older than the ex-miner and not at all robust,

Catcott shared a concern for the labouring poor; several of his poems are pleas on behalf of social victims and his outspokenness upset certain Wells citizens. He visited Harris in summer, probably during the early 1860's, and witnessed his Bible-reading forays. A wisp of romance sweetened his stay and years later he wrote of a certain maiden with whom he travelled called Ellen. Poets are heartless about satisfying our craving for vulgar specifics. We do not know where this summer rose came from, only that he met her "where the purple heather grows" and they journeyed by train to Falmouth and were delighted by the hospitality they received. He saw Harris as a poet-priest, a Biblical crusader who penetrated the gloomy dens where vice dwelt "in all its hideous hues". As Catcott was a bachelor, the poet's children provided him with a surrogate family. Little Alfred Harris, who combined a love of books with boyish glee, charmed him; he celebrated the boy's eighth birthday with a fulsome poem. When he became sick and frail, memories of Cornwall warmed his broodings:

> *Dark clouds are shading now*
> *My weary, aching brow,*
> *And wasting sickness, with her humbling hand,*
> *Has swept away the flowers*
> *That decked life's earlier hours*
> *And left me hoping for a better land.*
>
> *Yet still down in the West*
> *My spirit yearns to rest,*
> *Where loving hearts and kindred spirits dwell;*
> *And by some rippling rill,*
> *Near Ellen's dear old hill,*
> *My aching heart would sign its last farewell.*
> (Cornish Violets)

Harris's poem on Catcott was included in his next volume *Shakespeare's Shrine* (1866). This act of homage to his gifted predecessor was followed in 1868 by *Luda – A Lay of the Druids*, a kind of Dark Age melange, featuring a palmer, a Danish chieftain and a succulent Celtic maiden. The battle cry of the British warriors is "OUR HOME AND HEARTH!"

More telling perhaps is the essay in *Luda* dealing with yet another self-made singer, the shoemaker poet, Robert Bloomfield, born in Honnington, near Bury St. Edmunds, 1766. Entirely self-educated, Bloomfield worked on a farm and improved himself by purchasing a fourpenny dictionary and reading Shakespeare and Bunyan. While cobbling in poverty and squalor, he wrote *Farmer's Boy* which was not noticed until Mr Capel Lofft came to the rescue and issued it in quarto with illustrations by Bewick. *Farmer's Boy* sold twenty-six thousand copies and brought him money and fame. Bloomfield was one of those – dare one say it? – amiable souls who live blameless lives and write about it with luscious insipidity. Charles Lamb said that reading Bloomfield "makes me sick." Harris, on the other hand, felt a passionate empathy with the shoemaker and slipped in a timely plea for himself and other village Miltons:

"How many a humble toiler from the rustic cottage . . . dowered with the gift of genius, is left to languish and fall for the lack of timely aid which the affluent should rejoice to bestow! Should you ever have a child of song among you . . . one of humble origin and birth, whose hands are dignified with the dust of labour . . . encourage him by deeds of kindness, words of love and the purchase of his books . . ."

For connoisseurs of high coincidence, the high spot of *Luda* is the ingenuous yarn *Ralph Rind And His Son Seth*. Father, an out of work miner, is down on his luck and seems averse to positive thinking. "It's no use trying," said Ralph Rind, as he sat at the end of his table, whiffing the smoke from his pipe, lost in gloomy thought, which gave a melancholy expression to his wrinkled face.

"Is it not unmanly, dear Father," Seth chided, "to speak like this. Surely our great Father in heaven has sent us into this world to labour for one another . . ." There follows a lengthy rebuke which puts laggardly Ralph in his place.

The next day Ralph, inspired by Seth's garrulous piety, finds a Jew's House – a rich tin deposit – which alleviates his financial distress. Now Seth happens to love a comely maiden called Erno Eade whose parents will not consider him as a serious suitor owing to his poverty and lack of social standing. Fortunately there is a shipwreck. Seth goes down to the shore and sees a maid struggling in the waves. He rescues her and it turns out to be none other than Erno. She is admiring and grateful, but sadly her parents have been drowned in the shipwreck. Grasping that the obstacle to their happiness has been removed, Seth proposes. Erno accepts. They marry and Seth ends up a rich landed proprietor. One can picture Harris ruefully muttering as he finished this composition – "If only my problems would sort themselves out so easily!"

Illustration by John Alfred Harris

Chapter Twelve

Exodus and Death

The year of *Luda* (1868) was a year of Fenian unrest and revolution in Spain, leading to the dethronement of Queen Isabella. There was an attempt to shoot Prince Alfred, duke of Edinburgh, by an Irishman named O'Farrel, but he succeeded only in damaging the foot of an innocent bystander. Disraeli resigned, turning down a peerage for himself but accepting one for his wife.

The exodus of miners continued through the decade. According to *The West Briton* of May 18th, 1867, during the previous twelve months 7,380 of them left Cornwall, many finding jobs in the coal and iron mines of the North of England and some 1,155 settling in America. The Duchy's gnarled, acid-soiled hills had been blasted, drilled and tunnelled for centuries; it was a skeleton-land, picked clean of its mineral richness, and there was little sense in worrying it for yet more copper and tin when massive lodes lay unexplored on the other side of the world. Harris knew America to be a land of opportunities where wealth was distributed more evenly, but he never seriously considered emigration. Aside from one allusion in *My Mountain Home* to the possibility of "fate" commanding him to cross the seas, he seemed to have never considered seeking a fortune in the New World. The lure of profit made no impression upon him, unless it took the form of royalties gained from the sales of his books, which did not run above "a score or two of pounds." He was too contemplative, too wrapped up in the inner workings of his imagination. Several of his brothers had taken their mining skills across the Atlantic, but Harris was basically an armchair traveller.

In fact, he found the dream of America a source of inspiration.

Receiving letters from his brothers quickened his appreciation of the strangeness and spaciousness of the New World. As a young man, he had been transported by tales of dusky Indian maids and brave young warriors. These innocent savages were often the prey of brutal whites who used them for their own ends. His poem *Chanonchet and Wetamoe*, inspired by the verse-novels of Thomas Campbell, told the story of an Indian brave who was kidnapped and taken into slavery. He escaped and returned to camp but his love was missing:

> *But they have dragged my flower away,*
> *Turning to night my sunny day!*
> *My sweet wigwam, alas! is missing;*
> *The angry serpent there is hissing.*

America was also the home of the living poet he most admired, Henry Wadsworth Longfellow, who had a very slight correspondence with Harris. Longfellow sympathised with the Cornishman's hard life and literary ambitions. He was a man of sound principles who believed that poetry should ease the burden of living. Fond of elegiac nostalgias and soothing pieties, he ended his best-selling *Song of Hiawatha* with the appearance of Christian missionaries on the shores of Gitchi Gumee. Encircled by pipe-puffing Redskins, the Palefaces solemnly lecture them, not only on Jesus and the Virgin Mary, but also on how the Jews "mocked Him, scourged Him, crucified Him."

Such poetic high-mindedness stirred the Cornishman's heart. He sent Henry Wadsworth various volumes and the American in turn saluted his admirer across the seas:

MEN WHO HAVE RISEN
John Harris

The land of song within thee lies
Watered by living springs;
The lids of Fancy's sleepless eyes
Are gates unto that paradise:

Holy thoughts, like stars, arise;
Its clouds are angels' wings. – Longfellow.
(Quoted "Luton Times" 1876)

Another event which marked a threshold, a passing of an age, took place in May 1868. The corybantic (to steal the Reverend Shaw's well-chosen adjective) preacher Billy Bray died. Did Harris think, when he read of the passing of this little flame-quick evangelist, that one of the primal fires of Methodism had gone out? Billy's vitalism did not desert him at the end. Asked a few hours before his expiry whether he had any fear, his reply was as joyously whimsical as ever – "What! Me fear death! Me lost! Why, my Saviour conquered death. If I were to go down to hell, I would shout glory to my Blessed Jesus, until I made the bottomless pit ring again, and the miserable old Satan would say: Billy, Billy, this is no place for thee. Get thee back! Then up to heaven I would go shouting glory! glory! praise the Lord!"

But there were other deaths that affected Harris even more deeply. His mentor and subscriber, Captain Charles Thomas, passed away, a resolute servant of "King Jesus" to the end. George Smith of Trevu paid a handsome tribute to his fellow Methodee and society steward, preaching the sermon *The Christian Warrior Crowned*. Six years younger than Thomas, Smith barely outlived his friend, dying later in 1868.

George Smith's death was to have profound consequences for Harris, for he had taken a fatherly interest in the business side of Harris's publishing ventures, chivvying and enlisting subscribers. But now all the extra work fell on the poet. He lacked the business acumen of Smith. Separating people from their money is always a delicate business, and Harris found that religious poetry was not the most tantalising bait. "What a tug!" he exclaimed. "What a battle with the fates! What excuses! What refusals! What disdains!" The wealthy often turned their backs on his pleas, declining to purchase his latest volume, priced 2/6. "Nobody reads your books," one haughty gentleman informed, then stalked off to his dinner. These rejections cut Harris to the quick, for he had lived with almost painful frugality, denying himself small luxuries in order to cover the cost of printing.

*

Harris's next volume was *Bulo* which came out in 1871. It begins in a country residence by the sea, where Anleaf, the wife of a city merchant and her daughter, Bulo, are awakened by the serving-man, who introduces them to Walla, a shipwrecked mariner. Walla does not show exhaustion after his exertions, but treats his audience to a long, ethical lecture, in which one gets a glimpse of antipodean scenery:

> *The kangaroo*
> *Revels unscared along the river banks,*
> *Where the great emu sometimes comes to drink;*
> *Far off the gum trees nodded, their white trunks*
> *Gleamed in the sunset like the robes of saints*
> *And crimson parrots, green and snowy white,*
> *Whistled and shrieked among the winking leaves.*

Another personage, Tamson, the wife of a shrimp-catcher, observes, "I know that wonderful things happen nowadays: fire horses run upon wheels, men go up in the air in bladders, and love-letters are sent along the bottom of the sea . . . " It is not one of Harris's best pieces of writing; the upshot of ambition rather than intuition.

Destruction of the Cornish Tolmen has at least the virtue of positive indignation and most likely refers to Maen Rock, formerly at Constantine, an immense egg-shaped block about 33 feet long and resting on two stone supports, so that it resembled a passage-tomb. From Borlase's drawing, it seems to have been splendid and grimly imposing, an amazing natural folly until it was broken up in 1869. Harris was dismayed to hear that it had been charged and blasted by his fellow countrymen after surviving aeons and invasions. Those who should have been its guardians turned out to be its despoilers, for the sake of free stone posts and building material:

> *Anxious eyes,*
> *Stained deep with indignation, oft shall turn*
> *To scan the site it dignified for so long;*
> *And the wild bird, the haunter of the hills,*
> *Shall flounder in his passage, seeing not*

His ancient landmark: whirling round and round
In strange bewilderment, with shriek and cry
He'll leave the heights for ever.

Harris was a traditionalist, a lover of cottage tales and old ways; for him the tolmên symbolised the rude, unaffected faith of his forbears. In the brave new world of trains, velocipedes and telegraphs, he still clung to the values and objects he had loved as a child.

THE CONSTANTINE TOLMÊN OR MAEN ROCK,
THROWN DOWN MARCH, 1869.

The Constantine tolmên or Maen Rock, thrown down March, 1869.

Chapter Thirteen

The Bond of Peace

Harris had now passed his fiftieth birthday. Save for a tendency towards poetic flatuence, he showed no signs of lowering his standards; he retained his iron sense of duty, a truth-bearer to the end. However, middle-age had led him to an impasse. Although he found the seaport invigorating and his vocation rewarding, the life-and-death struggle had finished. Unyielding routine offered few insights beyond the knowledge that it was unlikely that he would ever attain the status of an independent man of letters. Always he would have to manage on meagre funds, Bible-reading till his throat was hoarse, soothing sickbeds, tramping back and forth from the Union workhouse, endlessly raising cash for new publications, fretting over poor delicate Alfred, trying to redeem a world more enamoured of profiteers than poets.

An important change in Harris's family came in 1871, when his daughter left home to marry. Her husband was Jonathan Wordsell whose father, also Jonathan, was a saddler, operating a business in Lower Market Street, Penryn, and in Market Street, Falmouth. Harris celebrated the event with a poem:

> *The Cornish child, the Cornish child*
> *Whose birthplace was the moorland wild . . .*
> *Has left her parents' roof today.*
> *O, for her and her partner pray.*

So began the first of six excruciating verses.

The year following (1872) saw an addition to the Harris clan, a grandson christened John Alfred Wordsell. One guesses Harris delighted in the baby boy and his sister, Beatrice, who was born two years later. Whether he liked his daughter's spouse is open to doubt, for Jonathan Wordsell turned out to be rather fly. A leather-worker by trade, originally he worked for his father, but later operated on his own account from 97 Killigrew Street. An advertisement was placed in the *Penryn Advertiser*, January 8th 1876, inviting respectable youths to apply "as apprentices to the Currying, also at Clicking in Boot Upper Trade . . ." The epithet "respectable" was to acquire an ironic dimension by November of the same year, when Wordsell absconded after being declared bankrupt and forging "a certain undertaking for payment of money, to wit, any dishonoured bill of the said J. Wordsell the younger." A reward of £50 was offered for the apprehension of the young felon, described as twenty-eight years old, five feet eight or nine inches high, of medium build, fair complexion, slight whiskers on the upper part of cheek, no moustache, a large mouth and prominent lips.

Most likely, this was a premeditated move. Wordsell absconded, then emigrated to America in October 1876, which must have proven highly distressing for Jane, who had the previous January given birth to a second son, Henry Howard Wordsell. Eventually she joined her husband, setting sail for America between October 1876 and September 1877. Harris missed his daughter. Women brought out his emotional side, and he imagined Jane sustained by her faith in a land of great forests and monotonous plains:

> *For she's gone, she is gone to the western land,*
> *Where the lakes are broad and the forests grand,*
> *To sing where the dark pines fringe the wild,*
> *"Lullaby, baby! sleep! sleep, my child!"*
>
> *But God is there, where the eagle soars,*
> *And the grand Niagara ever roars;*
> *Where the boundless prairie strangely swells,*
> *And the red man roams through pathless dells.*
> (The Last Lullaby – August 1877)

Initially Jane settled in Chicago, where she followed her father's example and ministered to the poor and sick. In 1894, she was awarded by the ladies of St. George Lodge, Chicago, a gold badge in the shape of a Roman Cross, together with a quilt presented by the ladies of St. Luke's Church guild. The presentation was a thanks-offering before she moved to Columbus, Ohio, and by 1897 she had settled in Brooklyn, where she was still in 1931. Of her subsequent relations with her husband, nothing is known. Back in Falmouth, Jonathan's brother, Henry Wordsell, took over the saddlery business in Lower Market Street, Penryn. Later he emigrated to the United States, almost certainly looking up Jonathan and Jane in Chicago, then moving on to Quincy, a manufacturing centre near Boston, finally coming to "a melancholy end" in 1898 when two tramps came across his frozen and dismembered body beside a railway track.

Aside from acquiring a son-in-law who fled rather than met his debts, Harris's years in Falmouth were exceptional in terms of the sheer quantity of verse he produced. His diatribes against the twin evils of war and drink increased, and he proved himself capable of such disconcerting felicities as rhyming "rat-tat" with "Nat". In 1872, he had brought out *Cruise of the Cutter*, a series of peace poems, dedicated to his faithful subscriber Baroness Burdett Couts, and written "to spread the principle of peace and accelerate in some humble way the desired consummation of the beating of swords into ploughshares and spears into pruning-hooks,* when men shall learn war no more."

Stimulus and support for such views were provided by Harris's close friend, John Gill, Quaker, pacifist and vegetarian. Gill edited the *Penryn Advertiser*, a small newspaper which he used to propagate his own liberal and religious opinions. He was a staunch friend to Harris, omitting the Wordsell scandal from his pages. Gill travelled up and down Britain, lecturing schoolchildren and peace groups, but on the Sundays when he was at home, he and Harris would sometimes attend the Society of Friends' meeting-house at Gyllyng Street, Falmouth. There is a photograph showing them together in Trevethan Lane: black-coated and black-hatted, they face each other like squat and bulky gnomes. Gill's arms hang loose; Harris grasps notebook and pencil as if he feels a poem stirring.

*Quoting the prophet Micah.

Being an ardent opponent of militarism, Gill could not ignore the dictates of his conscience. In defiance of the Lord Mayor of Penryn, he kept his office and bookshop open when the Duke of Wellington died. This enraged the curate-in-charge of St. Gluvias who waved his stick at the rebel. A bustling, likeable character, Gill was a stickler for his principles – he even objected to girls wearing red serge dresses, "the soldiers' colour." Convinced that tracts were the tools of social reform, he produced an unstoppable torrent of them – 228,000 in one year! Little can be said for this anti-war literature save that it possesses a bludgeon-like subtlety. After the fashion of the times, Gill portrays the fruits of war with exuberant revulsion.

"Imagine masses of coloured rags glued together with blood and brains," he wrote, "pinned into strange shapes by fragments of bone. Conceive men's bodies without heads, legs without bodies, heaps of human entrails attached to red and blue, disembowelled corpses in uniform, bodies lying about in all attitudes, with skulls shattered, faces blown off, hips smashed, bones, flesh and gay clothing all pounded together as brayed in a mortar . . ."

Reading this, one suspects that the tediously repetitive and gorily graphic battlefields of Harris's poems reflect Gill's outlook. By far the more politically sophisticated of the two, he urged Harris to write a series of 24 tracts called *Peace Pages*. He was kind enough to bring in Harris's invalid son, John Alfred, who illustrated the project – he had to work lying down owing to his bad back. John Alfred also wrote two peace tracts: *The Lifeboat* and *A Soldier's Story*. Harris was paid a pound for each four-page tract, which was generous for those days.

Such literature was both radical and admirable. Its argument was, that because war kills and maims and uses up funds which might be better employed feeding the hungry or building a hospital, international agreements should be drawn up to prevent it. The rightness of this is unassailable, and if ethics or morality always dominated human affairs, no doubt such attitudes could be enforced.

But eloquent pleas for social reform do not usually make great literature and Harris's desire to inculcate pacifist convictions in developing minds resulted in a crop of poems which have no merit beyond their intentions. Certain of his anti-war efforts, however, achieve a murky grandeur: epithets are spattered liberally and there is an appropriate amount of cannon-fire and haemorrhaging:

> *Shells burst and rockets hiss, and cannons roar,*
> *Death on his white horse rushes o'er the land,*
> *Trampling with iron hoofs the forms of men:*
> *Flames from his nostrils rush: proud chiefs are singed,*
> *Smouldering to ashes on his ruin-track.*
>
> *'Tis night: along the sky huge meteors walk*
> *Like giants flashing with mysterious blades.*
> *Behind them, on those clouds of gory red,*
> *Ride hosts of horsemen, and their flickering swords*
> *Clash and re-clash upon the ear of Night;*
> *And down the sides of those dark rolling hills*
> *Rush streams of human blood, with fire and smoke.*
>
> *On sweeps the war-fiend, on his car of flame,*
> *By hungry coursers drawn, whose iron teeth*
> *Gnash in their fury for a human meal.*
> *On sweeps the War-fiend, shaking his hot brand,*
> *With red hair streaming in the sulphur-blast,*
> *And visage dark with blood . . .*
> (The War Fiend)

Beside his proselytising and pamphleteering, Harris was carrying out an exacting schedule of work. A town missionary's life seems to have been no less arduous than a miner's. From the report of the Falmouth Scripture Readers' Society (1877), we learn that John Harris in the space of thirteen months paid 2105 visits to families, 1905 to the afflicted, held 143 cottage meetings, distributed 4282 tracts, visited the Union workhouse 26 times and the Maria Camilla Training School 27 times. Also he exchanged 700 library books, visited the Sailors' Home 122 times and attended the winter Soup Kitchen on 11 occasions. The quoted total is 1985 working hours – a mere 35-hour week! If those statistics are correct, Harris must have been a dazzling sprinter and his visits extremely brief. Probably walking time is not included.

However, living in the seaport had its compensations. Harris moved in a more exalted social milieu and he enjoyed the scenery and walks no less than the early trampings on the heights of Carn Brea. A favourite spot was the old church at Mylor, on the Carrick Roads, with its tall graveyard cross and tombs to drowned sailors. One evening he was rowed across to the granite building:

"Nought was heard but the dip of the oar of the boatman in the shining waters of the river, which slept at our feet like a sheet of crystal, as we wound our way down the sloping meads, on by sea-side, and then over the rural stile into the tree-covered church-yard . . . The darkness was made more palpable here by the shadows of the old trees, which cloaked us in their shrouds like the skirts of the god of gloom. We all involuntarily uncovered our heads from pure reverence . . . Tombs stood thick on the uneven sward . . . and seemed as if they were strangely watching our movements in the gathering darkness . . ."

Another excursion he took from Falmouth was in the company of a Quaker lady who affected the Biblical mode of address. "I should like to see thy birth-place, John Harris," she said. "Wilt thou be my guide to it?" Being sensitive to the charms of agreeable females, he agreed and they set off together by coach over the hills. The last half mile could not be done on wheels, so they stepped out and began to climb the side of the cairn, taking the route up Stoney Lane "over granite splinters, pebbles and small boulders, between hedges rich with golden furze, to what appeared to be the last human dwelling in creation." When they reached Harris's birthplace, they found it was all gone except for the foundations and fragments of wall. "The view from the old court was wide and wild," the Reverend Christophers wrote. "There were furzy and moorland valleys, and some of the most bare and bleak hills of the granite district: Carn Brea on one side, and on the other the breezy mountain undulations, over which lay the high road to Helston. The scene was inspiriting, with all its weird

97

loneliness. Nature, however, seemed to do honour to the poet, who had so honoured her. The primroses clustered by joyful crowds in the old deserted garden . . ."

A Falmouth character by John Alfred Harns

Chapter Fourteen

Local Heroics

During the 1870's the improvement in Harris's social status had the effect of altering his outlook. If not exactly a man of the world, he was now a long way from the lonely star-struck boy with his harp, bower and Bible. His inner eye was closing and the world was knocking at his door, making him adopt a social mask, take up causes and attitudes. Falmouth was more sophisticated than Camborne; as a port with international connections, it helped the poet to extend his horizons. It did not turn Harris into a political animal like his friend Gill, but it made him more aware of injustices that needed righting.

Harris had more faith in individuals than in parties or institutions. To him goodness was epitomised in the isolated acts of people he admired rather than in governmental decisions. But he was always prepared to apply his mind to the current affairs of his homeland. For instance, he wrote stories about the reclamation of waste land. It seemed appalling to him that so much money should be spent on weapons of destruction when moorland could be tilled, marshes drained and churches and hospitals built. In Cornwall, aided by steam ploughs, a fair amount of work had been done to this end. The burning of furze, the blasting of rock, the building of walls, had transformed the look of the countryside. In many instances, small patches of land had been set aside to provide gardens for the labouring poor. Lord Falmouth had gradually been enclosing his waste land and the Bassetts were quick to cultivate their own hitherto unproductive assets.

Another interest of Harris's was local acts of heroism, which provided material for occasional verses, and he mildly rebuked Tennyson for placing acts of valour in the past:

> *Gone is the age of knighthood,*
>   *The palfrey and the squire;*
> *And he who would revive it*
>   *Overstrains his lyre.*

He was inspired to write this after reading of the gallantry of Samuel Westlake who, on the 29th October 1872, averted a terrible accident. A train laden with 150 tons of china clay left Burngullow station about 4.40 p.m. It was scheduled to stop at St. Austell but it roared past the station towards Par. The passengers on the platform were horrified. Cornwall Railway was single-line. Another engine – the mail train driven by Westlake – had just left Par and was approaching the runaway engine. About one mile from St. Austell, Samuel Westlake identified the hazard and blew the brake whistle. Instead of jumping for safety, he stopped and reversed the engine, running backwards at full speed towards Par chased by the china clay train. At one point the engines came within twenty yards of one another. Fortunately the mail train pulled ahead and entered Par station and shuffled to a halt. The passengers showered gifts and compliments on their clear-headed driver.

Although it is a fine thing that such presence of mind should be honoured, Harris's verses lack the virtues of vivid reportage and are not quite bad enough to challenge the immortal banalities of William MacGonagall:

> *He blanched not at the prospect,*
>   *He leaped not from his stand;*
> *The mighty, moving engine,*
>   *Obeyed his master hand*
> *And backward turned in triumph,*
>   *Still followed by the foe,*
> *Which rushed along the incline*
>   *With sounds of instant woe.*

> *Still Westlake faced the danger*
> *And coolly kept his place,*
> *Forcing the mail train backwards,*
> *Till he outran the chase,*
> *And safely reached the station;*
> *With all his charge complete,*
> *Who thronged around the driver,*
> *With thanks and praises meet.*

Samuel Westlake was not the only knight of steam honoured by Harris. When a carriage caught alight, presumably from the heat of the engine, another heroic driver, Joseph A. Sieg, managed to stop the train, burning himself but saving the passengers:

> *Six hundred lives were granted him*
> *In answer from above,*
> *Six hundred lives for one grand act,*
> *Then his went out in love*
> *But honour shall adorn his tomb,*
> *Where flowers of freedom lean,*
> *The lily and the forget-me-knot,*
> *With everlasting green.*

*

By 1874, he felt able to view his work in critical retrospect. He decided to appraise and classify his poems according to theme and subject matter and put them before the public. So he took the plunge and brought out his most comprehensive selection *Wayside Hymns, Pictures and Poems*, a sumptuous quarto volume, double-columned, with a frontispiece photograph of the author looking mild-eyed and benevolent. The burden of distribution was alleviated by Robert Alexander Grey, a gentleman who disposed of more than £50's worth of copies. *Wayside Pictures* is not an easy collection to read. In condensed print the poetic dramas seem even more gaseous, and the glibly tripping lines of the sentimental ditties even more vacuous. Powerful and idiosyncratic writing is there but it is often robed in windy rhetoric.

The autobiographical element is strong. In fact, the problem of Harris's career is implicit in the book, an element of what one could call experience-starvation. His life can be divided into two almost equal halves: first the harsh, exciting years as a miner, when he revelled in love, scenery and domestic joys; second the move to Falmouth and the stabilisation of his status as poet and preacher.

Initially, after casting off his miner's chains and setting down new roots, he had felt an overwhelming relief. This was inevitably followed by a sense of disconnection. For all of his deepest passions, his profoundest commitments, his griefs and delights, had been lived out amid the rearing pitheads and granite fields of Carn Brea. He found himself forever sifting through the detritus of memory and reaching back to his more vital core. When loss touched him, he would relapse into a kind of poignant haze and imagine that he was a young man again, holding Lucretia by the hand and leading her through the Reenes, a wooded valley between Troon and Pendarves, or across the Bolenowe meadow called the Under Field:

> *The hum of insects met my ear,*
> *The gorse in gold was dressed,*
> *And underneath the hawthorn near*
> *The robin built its nest;*
> *The lark his sweetest song did yield,*
> *Which fell in liquid showers:*
> *O, nought was like the Under Field*
> *All white with daisy flowers.*
>
> *Nor will it fade from memory's eye,*
> *From memory's treasured store,*
> *Till darkness shadows earth and sky,*
> *And life itself is o'er.*
> *A bliss by hidden hands unsealed,*
> *To cheer my latest hours,*
> *Is that hill-sloping Under Field*
> *All white with daisy flowers.*

(From Harris's "Autobiography")

Wayside Pictures did not mark a break in Harris's prolific output. He continued to write journalism mixed with verse, always with an instructional or preaching slant, culminating in a collection of assorted pieces, *Tales and Poems* (1877), which had previously appeared in weekly serials. John Alfred again provided the illustrations of quaint rural figures, horses, orphans and drooping foliage. They are naive and slightly clumsy, yet with an undeniable appeal, and one can almost share the young man's pride in his work. Fearing the criticism of others, Harris felt obliged to draw attention to the "imperfect pictures" as if an apology was necessary.

Tales and Poems comprises mainly prose pieces. The tales are eloquently told but they are no more than vehicles for moral judgements. "I have not had quite enough bread for breakfast, mother," said little Frank Fraddon in *Frank Fraddon and his Father*; "but I shall thank God, nevertheless, for it is more than I deserve." This infant paragon is not very believable – Lord Fauntleroy seems a monster of selfishness by comparison! More fun is the boisterous braggart Flavel Roberts, who always says "I know better" and walks over a precipice while ignoring his good wife Eleanor's advice. Even better is the tale of Walter Whear and his cow Brindle. Particularly moving is the manner in which his wife, Martha, addresses the good-natured beast: "Brindle, I love you. You are the sleekest of cows, as quiet as a summer lake, and just as pure. Your crumpled horns are handsome, so are your back and sides and your nose has no compare . . ."

Genuine social indignation flashes out here and there. Harris shows his radical colours in *Ally Ardwick, the Barm Seller* (barm was the old name for yeast) dealing with an old couple who are forced to enter the workhouse where they will occupy separate apartments:

"They had lived together as man and wife upwards of forty years; and now, when they really need each other's sympathy most, when poverty had come upon them like an armed man . . . they are to be severed from each other. Heaven will surely, sooner or later, avenge this great insult against His high command. How would the squire, or the parson, or the burly magistrate, appreciate such a disaster brought upon themselves . . . Shame on Christian England to

sanction such a sin! How long will those who sit in the high places of the earth wilfully shut their eyes and ears to the wrongs of the poor?"

Another tale *Ben the Basket-Maker* reveals his contempt for the pageantry of the hunt. Fat, scowling Squire Spratt and his doubletted henchmen gallop forth in jingling finery to pursue the innocent hare:

"See how the dear little thing leaps, and jerks, and bounds from shallow to shallow, steaming with perspiration. And after it still bellow the horsemen and hounds, with unjust ardour burning in their breasts, thirsting for the blood and bones of a poor defenceless brute!"

The poet expostulates:

"Shame, shame, ye landed autocrats; vent your spleen on the giant destroyers of our race – adultery, fornication, uncleanness, lasciviousness, idolatry, witchcraft, hatred, variance, emulations, wrath, strife, seditions, heresies, envyings, murders, drunkenness, revellings, and such like, and leave the poor dumb, innocent beast untortured, so that the cry of the hounds be heard no more in this land. Instead of your lavish expenditure on your dogs and steeds, allow us to suggest that you feed the hungry, clothe the naked, and treat the daily labourer with due consideration . . .[†]*"*

When the subject roused him, Harris must have been a treat to listen to. His forward-looking principles and broad and humane range of sympathies do him credit. Even today one hears people dismissing the element of barbarity in such activities and it is cheering to find a poet in remote Cornwall over a century ago speaking up so frankly. Often the poet's indignation or enthusiasm was awakened by casual reading: *Irving's Noble Act* is an account (The Times, September 1876) of how a poor factory operative was saved by a medical student who donated twenty-five ounces of his blood. The patient's leg had been amputated; only an infusion could save him:

Nothing could save the factory man from dying
  But blood and blood alone,
Who almost pulseless in the ward was lying
  When IRVING gave his own.

  Which inevitably recalls the greatest blood-sacrifice of history –
"One who died for all."

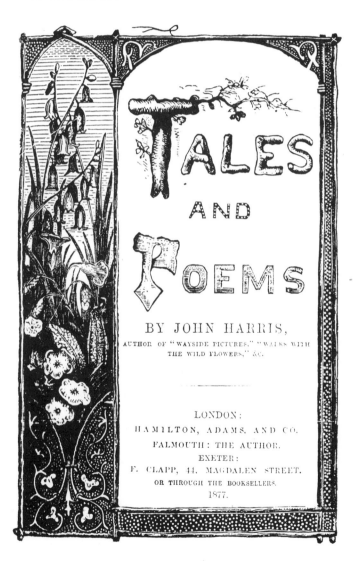

TALES AND POEMS

BY JOHN HARRIS,

AUTHOR OF "WAYSIDE PICTURES," "WALKS WITH
THE WILD FLOWERS," &c.

LONDON:
HAMILTON, ADAMS, AND CO.
FALMOUTH: THE AUTHOR.
EXETER:
F. CLAPP, 44, MAGDALEN STREET.
OR THROUGH THE BOOKSELLERS.
1877.

Chapter Fifteen

The Two Giants

Between the months of December 1877 and April 1878, Harris was preparing the manuscript of his thirteenth volume of poems, *The Two Giants.* Over a thousand pounds, he announced, had been invested in publishing ventures, "a serious sum to be accounted for by a working man." The collection opened with a prefatory poem to Lord Northbrook.

> *The truest helper is the man of peace,*
> *Whose sword is sheathed, whose spear is idly pent,*
> *Who strives that war and wretchedness may cease,*
> *The gun be hushed, and the last bullet spent;*
> *To save, not waste, his sanctified intent:*
> *Who cheers his brother on life's rude highway,*
> *Whose feeble steps are slowly homeward bent.*
> *And such is NORTHBROOK, with no false display,*
> *So gladly I inscribe to him my simple lay.*

"It will be obvious to the reader," Harris wrote in the introduction, "that the two huge overgrown monsters herein personified, and giving the book its title, are none other than GIANT DRINK and GIANT WAR, whose terrible deeds so desolate the earth. They both destroy their thousands and their tens of thousands of all ages: and the writer trusts that these simple lyrics, which are chiefly scenes of rural life, and pictures from the toiling peasantry of the realm, may be welcomed by his philanthropic countrymen, and serve, in some small measure, to accelerate the overthrow of INTEMPERANCE and the

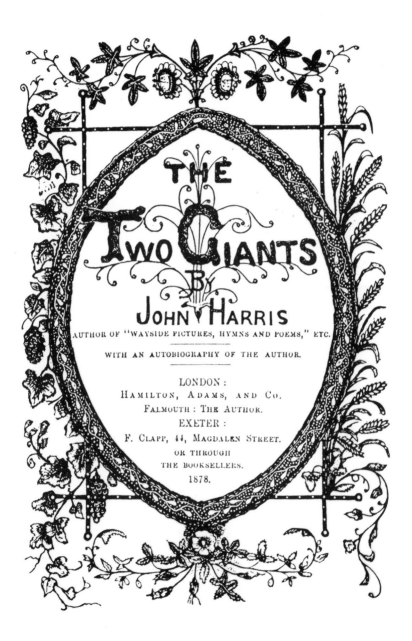

THE
TWO GIANTS
BY
JOHN HARRIS
AUTHOR OF "WAYSIDE PICTURES, HYMNS AND POEMS," ETC.

WITH AN AUTOBIOGRAPHY OF THE AUTHOR.

LONDON:
HAMILTON, ADAMS, AND CO.
FALMOUTH: THE AUTHOR.
EXETER:
F. CLAPP, 44, MAGDALEN STREET.
OR THROUGH
THE BOOKSELLERS.
1878.

SWORD." Attached to the volume is an autobiographical sketch, describing the trials of his arduous life.

There is something almost alarming about the prominent capitals. True, they had become a typographical convention, but it seems as if Harris has ceased writing for mature adults and is instead concentrating on a Sunday school audience. The level of writing seldom rises above naive doggerel and indifferent verse. How could the man who wrote the exquisite lines to Lucretia devote so much energy and expense to such fourth-rate material? On a purely technical level, the verses against war and drink fail; the triteness of the rhymes destroys the gravity of the message. If these lines had been written by Thomas Hood, they would have been regarded as sophisticated parody:

> "*I think I'll ope the wicket,*
> *And hobble to the door,*
> *And stand beneath the woodbine,*
> *A knocking as of yore.*"
> *And soon he looked on Fanny,*
> *Alas! Another's bride;*
> *And in a few weeks after*
> *Poor crippled Willie died.*
> (Crippled Willie)

While another opening suggests an impure limerick:

> *On the broad railway platform stood Jonathan Block,*
> *With a face full of sadness, awaiting his Jock . . .*

Even the names Harris selects – to ensure memorability perhaps? – are rather odd. Who would want to be called Elihu Burritt, Zebedee Zog, Aaron Arch, Jeremy Jeer, Watt Willow, Solomon Sloop, Nancy Nacoo or Bess Blew? The embarrassment of owning to such titles would secure a childhood of tantrums and tears. No wonder several ended their lives in drink and darkness.

In his capacity as a miner and a gospel-reader, Harris had witnessed scenes of appalling poverty. He had endured sickness and food-shortage and lived through an era in which Britain had become involved in a number of foreign wars. Yet part of him was intellectually divorced from reality. Believing that the Christian gospel represented the noblest fruit of human endeavour, he was incapable of seeing that his verse-sermons could only have a limited appeal. It did not occur to him that certain messages can be true and just without being particularly profound or interesting.

Also, there was an element of vanity in the enterprise. Like other writers, Harris had become print-mad and begun to repeat himself, drawing attention to his piety, his simplicity and perseverance. He was forced to sell the myth of himself as the miner who made good, in the same way that a fashionable actor finds himself playing basically the same parts again and again, for fear of disappointing or failing to attract his regular audience. Considering the large sums of money needed to publish and distribute the poems, his one-man campaign of obsessional intensity was probably necessary.

Harris mixed mostly with sober middle-class mentors, who liked to see sentimentality in verse rather than vigour or originality. He saw them as his social superiors and, more unfortunately, his literary mentors. They praised his work when it promoted Christianity and censured drink and violence, for their province was self-improvement rather than poetry. As Arthur Langford* has observed, under the auspices of Gill and others, Harris was "actually being paid for writing, which was so different from writing speculatively where he could take the time to alter and polish at will." No longer was he sole master of his subject matter; "self-expression and inspiration were being sacrificed to the treadmill of mass production."

Lord Northbrook, to whom Harris dedicated his *Walks With Wild Flowers* (1875), was a more consequential fish than Gill, a statesman of international repute, who, in 1881, secured a grant of £100 from the Civil List for the poet. Northbrook entered parliament as a Liberal M.P. for Falmouth and Penryn, later serving as under-secretary of state for India. In this capacity, he averted the calamity of the Bengal famine by refusing to stop the import of grain and increasing the import of rice.

*In his notes on the present MS.

'Neath the boughs,
With rich fruit laden, many a parent's lips
Shall murmur forth his deed, and bless his name,
Who filled their rice-bowl in the day of dearth . . .
(Peace Pages)

The above is quoted in the *Penryn Advertiser*, July 1876, sandwiched between accounts of the Turkish war, the National Temperance Fête and a fatal accident in a hay field, when an unfortunate Mr Mayne slid off his waggon, falling in a sitting posture and dying instantly.

In the context of patrons, another name crops up in Harris's writings, Baroness Burdett Coutts (1814–1906), to whom *The Cruise of the Cutter* is dedicated. She is hailed for her "Christian consideration to the toilers of Great Britain" and as "a benefactress of mankind" (and therefore presumably of Harris himself). Tall, slender, graceful and grave, the Baroness was described as the "richest heiress in all England." When she inherited part of Thomas Coutts banking fortune, no eligible young man was said to have abstained from proposing to her. Her philanthropic enterprises were vast and comprehensive and she endowed churches, schools, hospitals, museums and scientific institutions. Unfailingly energetic and considerate, at one time she enjoyed a fame second only to Queen Victoria whose Coronation she attended in Westminster Abbey. Most of her work was conducted from her address in Stratton Street, Piccadilly, but she did visit Cornwall, buying in 1865 the geological collection of Edward Lavin of the Egyptian House, Penzance, and donating it to the University Museum, Oxford. Every right-thinking man in the realm craved the attention of the Baroness, and, on a purely literary level, Harris had to compete with Charles Dickens who thought her "an excellent creature" and dedicated *Martin Chuzzlewit* to her. Harris thought highly of her because she combined Croesian riches with a sense of Christian duty. In the poem *Davie Drake*, the eponymous hero is born in a humble moorland cottage, yet by dint of sobriety, piety and hard work, he reaches the top:

At last he reached the golden height
With streaks of glory laden:
He gained the Lily of the Loch,
The banker's matchless maiden.

Such lines would make a strong Marxist weep, yet one cannot help wondering whether the "banker's matchless maiden" was a discreet tribute to Angela Georgina Baroness Coutts.

THE SWEET BRIER.

Illustration by John Alfred Harris from 'Walks with Wild Flowers'

111

Chapter Sixteen

A Poetic Autobiography (1879)

For about ten years, Harris had been writing fluent and copious poetic journalism, lacking observation or insight, a world of trite tragedies and cardboard rhymes. The verse neither touched the base-rock of everyday life nor that spiritual reality which it strained to celebrate. At last, the inner eye opened and he began to write his poetic autobiography *Monro*, probably his smoothest and most accomplished poem. Poverty more often gives rise to hack-work than to masterpieces, and the key to the revival of Harris's creative powers was probably a greater financial stability, which gave him freedom to pursue the themes closest to his heart. He had been awarded a grant of £50 per annum from the Royal Literary Fund (1873–5) and a one-time grant of £200 from the Royal Bounty Fund, April 1877.

He cast *Monro* in Spenserian stanzas, a form which allows for a considerable flexibility of mood – pensive, dramatic and descriptive. It is a prolonged, calm meditation on the life of a low-born miner who sets out to serve both Jesus and poetry. Harris often picks out significant names and *Monro* could be a tribute to Edward Monro (1815–1866), a preacher and religious writer popular at the time. The poem is the apotheosis of Harris, celebrating Cornwall, domesticity, moral courage, nature and God. Lacking the energetic fatalism of *Carn Brea*, the storm-exulting grandeur, it is perhaps truer to the essential spirit of the miner-poet. By temperament he was always "a sweet singer" and his central subject matter was himself. All the themes and memories which had been running through the rhyme-mill of his mind are maturely worked into *Monro*: his childhood, youth, marriage,

The startled sun grew dark at fervid noon,
   The great hills rocked like boulders in their bed,
The cattle lowed to be called home too soon,
   And thunder spoke to thunder overhead.
Sheeted and pale, up rose the buried dead; [whine;
   Rocks crashed, and voices through the valleys
The temple's veil was rent like slender thread,
   And those who in the Saviour's death combine
Confessed with burning lips He was the King Divine.

And through the universe an echo rolled,
   Re-echoing still when stars are on the deep,
Or the sun shines in all his wealth of gold
   On the green pastures, or the barren steep;
In isles remote where palms in silence sleep,
   And waters wash the yet untrodden shore,
Where torrents tumble to the wild bird's sweep,—
   " 'Tis finished! He sin's ruin doth restore,
And to believing man opes wide heaven's golden
     door."

Extract and illustration from 'Monro' (1879)

113

mining experiences, visit to Stratford and experience of becoming a Bible-reader. In places it is lush, exuberant and overflowing, but then so was the inner vision of the poet.

At the poem's core, like a fire in the hearth, sits the stable and loving family who were the mainstay of his life. Harris had no misgivings about praising the Bible, family life and home-cooking. The narration in *Monro* has a reflective, yet discernible momentum, and the more complex rhyming scheme keeps glibness at bay. The poet's credo is expressed with admirable clarity:

> *The loftiest labour man can e'er perform,*
> *Is that which tends to mitigate distress;*
> *To shield bereavement from the biting storm.*
> *And make oppression's iron fetters less . . .*

We see the miner wielding a sledgehammer, sweating at the mineral vein, wiping his forehead, pencilling verses upon his iron wedge. He feels overawed by the vast and threatening interior:

> *The cavern's sides, the vagues of shining spar,*
> *The roof of rock where scarce the candle gleams,*
> *The hollow levels strangely stretching far*
> *Beneath the mountain, full of mineral seams . . .*

> *Oft would he stand upon some splintered spar*
> *Surcharged with wonder, gazing in the gloom;*
> *And weird eyes seemed to watch him from afar,*
> *And bending bipeds through the blackness loom.*

Which is contrasted with wholesome family life:

> *At supper-time, when sitting round the board,*
> *His joy was greater than the spear has won;*
> *The jug of milk, the seed-cake from the hoard,*
> *And now, perchance, the pie or currant-bun.*

And then there are the moments of profound silence, when nature closes round him and he feels near to God. Harris never expressed an opinion about Wordsworth – perhaps he disliked the older man's pantheism – but he surely must have understood him. Few have better   expressed those keen and chilling moments of solitary joy:

> *And when the hush is deepest, and the moors*
> *   Stretch away beneath the lofty sky,*
> *Where quiet Evening folds her dusky doors,*
> *   And on the marsh is heard the heron's cry,*
> *No human face, no habitation nigh,*
> *   Man, holding converse with his inner life,*
> *Learns how to live, and better, how to die,*
> *   And God Himself draws near to still the storm of strife.*

The poem closes with a death-wind rippling across a sea. Monro is waiting in a rocking boat, almost impatient to be drawn into the current of eternity.

> *His task is ended, and he feels like one*
> *   Whose boat is rocking 'neath the island trees,*
> *Where gorgeous birds are fluttering in the sun,*
> *   And harps ring sweetness on the sauntering breeze . . .*

Harris sent *Monro* across the Atlantic to Henry Wadsworth Longfellow, the contemporary poet he idolized. The other replied from Cambridge (Mass.) on January 13th, 1880:

"I shall read this volume with deep interest and sympathy; for I see by the preface and by the argument of the several books, that it is your life. The thought uppermost in my mind at this moment is, what a divine gift the benediction of song must have been to you through all your laborious life. How dark your way would have been without it! How luminous it has been with it!"

One senses that Longfellow was not altogether transported. He restricted his praise to Harris's indomitable perseverance. His reaction was similar when he was sent a copy of *Wayside Pictures, Hymns and Poems*. While offering to get the poems noticed by the American press, he shuns the grubby arena of criticism.

If Longfellow's reaction was cautious, the English press

showered Harris with unanimous praise. Even literary periodicals like *The Athenaeum*, known for the acidity of its reviews, handled the ex-miner gently. There must have been some attacks as well, but sensibly enough Harris did not include them among the commendations that append his collections. The poet is complimented on his "lovely fancies and liquid music" and assured a place among the singers of the day. Quoting long, verbose reviews rapidly becomes monotonous, especially when most employ an identikit Victorian phraseology, but here is a sampler of typical comments:

"It is the very book for the season – fresh as April, sweet as May, and rich as the flowers and melodies of June."
("West Briton" reviewing "Tales and Poems", 1878)

"No man can read these poems without rising from their perusal a better man. A beautiful contentment shines from every page. Would that every king were like this man! We are loath to part from these poems which are so homely and so ennobling . . ."
("The Critic" reviewing "Tales and Poems")

"Mr Harris has written verses which, compared with those of some ardent claimants on the public purse, are as the wine of flowers to the stagnant water of a froggy pool."
("The Athenaeum" reviewing "Tales and Poems")

These refer to one volume alone. But their general tone is repeated elsewhere. Harris is compared to Burns, Longfellow and Robert Bloomfield. The "many stirring pieces and pathetic lyrics" are recommended to "lovers of green fields and meadow brooks." It is all very comforting and salubrious and therefore it comes as rather a surprise to find a dissenter in the guise of the squarson, Sabine Baring Gould, who launched at attack on Harris in his book on Cornish worthies.

Baring Gould's posthumous essay on Harris is based almost exclusively on extracts from the autobiography. He finds "no vital spark" in the poet's work; no residual core of intelligent perception. "He called himself the miner poet," the squarson concludes, "but he is not even a minor poet. There is something pathetic in the contemplation of a man of this sort. I have come across several men – men who have a love of nature, an appreciation of the good and true, but have no genius, no originality, who can imitate but create nothing."

There is some force in this argument – Harris was no thinker – but it ignores the marvellous descriptive power of *Carn Brea* and the moving impact of his elegiac poetry. Admittedly, when one considers the quantity of inferior work he produced, it is easy to forget that Harris was ever struck by the lightning of inspiration. It would be possible for this book to be cast as a biography of a pious miner, who, deluded by the praise of middle-class mentors, believed that he was a profound religious poet and turned his life into a fanatical campaign of self-promotion, resulting in volume after volume of handsomely bound mundanities.

Illustration from 'Monro' by John Alfred Harris

Chapter Seventeen

The Scripture Reader

In Falmouth the poet became a familiar sight, returning to or going from the headquarters of the Union, where they kept in compulsory employment the old, the poor and the ailing. Union houses were formed after the Poor Law Amendment Act of 1834 which closed the small parish workhouses and replaced them with large, regimented ones. They became extremely unpopular and were decried as "Bastilles". It was Harris's job to give moral uplift to the inmates of workhouses and other charitable institutions.

Bible in hand, sober-suited, with a pronounced forward bend of the head, Harris would tread the streets and alleys of the port, knocking on doors and trying to interest anyone in the teachings of the Man from Bethlehem. He had a broad, round face and a bushy surround of grey whiskers offset by a bald head. His blue eyes were frank and friendly; his manner kindly and unaffected. If the subject of poetry was broached, his expression took on an eager glow and his speech would become rapider and gestures more flamboyant. One lady announced on seeing him, "Behold, the dreamer cometh," to which Harris replied, "I may appear absent-minded sometimes." People observed that he seldom noticed passers-by but kept his eyes fixed on the ground. The ageing Harris was a pavement-gazer rather than a straight-backed patrician like Alfred Lord Tennyson.

His friendliness and goodwill impressed many poor people in Falmouth, but inevitably in some places he was met with abuse and ordered to leave. This was painful to his sensitive nature, especially as he considered it his duty to persist, to return to the place where he had been rebuked or insulted. One woman was very antagonistic; for many months she persecuted him with shouting and raillery, but he continued to address her civilly, until the virago had a change of heart and welcomed him into her home. From that moment they became friends, and he was always assured of a warm reception. He became a familiar figure who was treated with familiarity. Children waited for him in the streets because he was usually armed with free tracts and leaflets, although more often than not, they might be used for making paper darts or boats. Under stones by the wayside, on roadside seats, in bustling and deserted places, he dropped these messages of peace and salvation.

In many homes he became popular. Old people, in particular, took to the poet and liked to express their gratitude by giving him small presents or keepsakes. He would acquire objects like an antique box, a bit of jewellery or an ebony elephant brought from the East by an old sailor. He did not want these items, but his refusal to take them might result in tears, so he acquiesced.

Some of the places he visited were squalid in the extreme. He entered lightless attics where down-and-outs slept swathed in sacking or dragged out their lives in rat-infested cellars. He came across drunken men who slurred obscenities at him and men who made strange confessions concerning the felonies they had committed in the past. They disclosed things horrible enough to make the hearer shudder, but Harris bore it all with fortitude and restraint. He visited the sick-ward of the workhouse and elicited more histories, chronicles of decline and fall, which he incorporated into his poetry.

Setting this down, one is conscious of taking Harris's testimony on trust? Can we believe that he was always so patient, so obliging, so tenaciously pious with the social rejects he visited? Did he never turn on these people or lose his temper? Probably not – it is likely that he was simply being honest when he presents himself as impervious to anger or irritation. The Christian qualities – of quiet sufferance and turning the other cheek – had become an ingrained reaction. If we discount the ludicrous braggadocio of the 'wizard' and his magic onions (the only muscular confrontation with the forces of darkness he bothered to record), we must accept that forty years of preaching had taught him to deflect hostility and cynicism. To insult Harris and his faith was merely to provoke him to be extra mild and considerate. And he had over the years developed the ability to listen and absorb even while being rebuked. This was useful when he began to weave the lives of down-on-outs into dramatic tapestries.

Testimonies of these unfortunates were not literally transcribed. Instead they were dressed up in bardic robes and transformed by the alchemy of language. Illiterate, drunken oafs appraise their decline and fall with long-winded dignity. The poem *Caleb Cliff* probably originated in the stews of Falmouth. At the centre of the drama is a stereotypical Victorian no-gooder who spurns the Bible and good advice, succumbing instead to vast quantities of alcohol. Neglecting his loving wife and children, he sneers at the pietistic traveller and declares:

> *Drink, more drink!*
> *Why should I care if others swim or sink?*

However, during the course of a long inebriated blank-verse discourse, he suffers an attack of delirium tremens:

> *Round my head*
> *Whirl fiery circles, and the moor is full:*
> *Imps with long tongues are licking at my brow,*
> *And snakes with wings of flames crawl up my breast:*
> *Huge monsters glare upon me, some with horns,*
> *And some with hoofs that blaze like pitchy brands.*
> *Great trunks are some, and some are hung with heads.*
> *Here serpents dash their stings into my face*
> *All tipped with fire; and there a wild bird drives*
> *His red-hot talons in my burning scalp.*
> *Here bees and beetles buzz about my ears*
> *Like crackling coals, and frogs strut up and down*
> *Like hissing cinders: wasps and water-flies*
> *Scorch deep like melting mineral. Murther! save!*
> *What shall a sinner do?*

Whereupon Caleb repents his drunkenness and is led home to his wife by the traveller, who urges him to read the Bible.

The imagery is worthy of Revelation and Hieronymus Bosch. The grotesque beasts are a fearful distraction and the marching

Against the demon drink – John Alfred Harris

frogs dreadful and funny at the same time. A more curious detail is the bird attacking the scalp, which had previously appeared at the end of *Carn Brea*. One wonders whether Harris, whose hair was mainly concentrated around his chin, felt vulnerable in this region.

Caleb Cliff amply demonstrates that Harris's views on drinking were censorious. It seems that he had never once succumbed to even mild inebriation, believing that the road to hell was marked by tavern signs. In actual fact, in the early days the moderate consumption of beer and wine was not discouraged at Quarterly Meetings and other Wesleyan functions. In Harris's home town, Camborne, there still stands "a small, squat building" which belonged to the Teetotal Methodists, a branch which reached Cornwall in 1837. Probably Harris was influenced by this group whose tenets gradually gained broad acceptance, though some took the opposite view, maintaining that Jesus drank wine occasionally and did not condemn it. "There was a good deal of strong feeling on the subject," wrote Thomas Shaw, "and it was often intemperately expressed. A wag at the Wesleyan conference raised a laugh by saying that Cornish Methodism was in a state of fermentation . . ."

Many reformers had previously expressed the view that sordid living conditions stunted the moral development of the poor, and that drink provided the only respite from miserable occupations and surroundings. George MacDonald wrote of "ragged women who took their half-dead babies from their bare, cold, cheerless bosoms and gave them of the poison which they themselves drank renewed despair in the name of comfort . . . Where do they all go when the gin-halls close their yawning jaws? Where do they lie down at night? In the charnel vaults of pestiferously crowded lodging houses, in the prisons of police stations, under the dry arches within hoardings."

These lamentable sights gave impetus to the many temperance groups in Victorian Britain. Denying oneself alcohol became an active virtue rather than an expression of personal inclination and institutions were founded whose principal attractions were an absence of drinkable refreshment. The fluctuating economy of Cornwall created conditions where extreme abstinence and swaggering indulgence went side by side. Many miners, for instance, were the epitome of raucous drunkenness while their Methodist colleagues were often as stiff and sober as statues. But as the century progressed, ideas of moderation gained increasing acceptance and non-drinkers consolidated their foothold in Falmouth in April 1872, when a Teetotal Public House was opened in Swanpool Street which was announced as being:

A Public-House without the drink
Where men can sit, talk, read, and think,
Then safely home return.

Newspapers and various periodicals were provided along with tea, coffee and other provisions. Perhaps Harris himself snatched an odd half-hour's relaxation in this high-intentioned canteen between Bible-reading sessions.

Chapter Eighteen

Last Lays

The final phase of Harris's life was a busy one. He maintained his output of poetry and authors sent him books in exchange for his own. His library grew more extensive and erudite, and early in 1879 he was elected a Fellow of the Royal Historical Society. Also, he was gratified to receive a Civil List grant of £100, September 1881, from Mr Gladstone, through the efforts of Earl Northbrook and R. Webber. He had lost a large portion of a previous £200 grant from the Royal Bounty Fund by investing it in the Cornish Bank which closed on New Year's Day, 1879. Investors were offered 16 shillings in the pound compensation at a meeting in Truro which John Gill – another unlucky investor – attended.

By now, his contribution had become part of the history of Methodism. The Reverend Christophers's book *Poets of Methodism* had given him a flattering mention. It tells the story of a miner, who is tempted by his friends to desert his family and go to South America and seek his fortune. He ponders what is the right thing to do. Then he reads a hymn written by a man who had been a miner at Dolcoath like himself: *The Lord Shall Choose For Me* by John Harris. The Lord decides that he must abide at home. As for his comrades, they went to South America and "made their fortunes, as the people say, but lost their souls."

Such anecdotes were treasured by Harris because they bolstered his self-image. Judged objectively, his life could hardly be classed as a failure: all of his work had attained the permanence of hard covers, unlike that of Gerard Manley Hopkins (1844–89), whose poems had to be posthumously issued through the agency of

Robert Bridges. But there was no steady growth of Harris's reputation, and after the flare-path of his early success and the winning of the Shakespeare Prize, not a great deal had happened to enhance his standing. Hence, like many neglected writers, he revelled in compliments, even those extolling his respectability rather than his poetry. "Unlike many Scottish poets who consider tippling a concomitant to genius," a Dr. Rogers told him, "you have conducted yourself well, and gained public favour both as a man and as an author."

Another bonus was the acquisition of a study – a small enough privilege, one might think, for a man of letters who had waited since he was a child. From the Royal Literary Fund grant of £50, he had a room built over his kitchen, which was completed in October 1874. He had plenty of work to occupy him, notably a serial of 63 chapters, *Mountain Mat and his Three Sons*, which was bought by Mr J.E.M. Vincent, editor of two Leamington weeklies. His elder son, James Howard, provided a glimpse of his father in his retreat. "His little fire is attended to; the lamp sheds its light through the chamber, and he commences to write. A book with a scrap of stout paper or old book-cover set upright shades his eyes from the glare of the light, and throws its beam on the paper held in his hand. Sitting in his chair with well-worn quill or long-worked steel pen, he is busily employed in inditing the poem that has been composed during the evening. Perhaps, in the midst of his verse-writing, a summons from some dying man arrives to draw him aside for the time to encounter the stern realities of our frail humanity."

While sitting in the study one day in April 1878, his body went numb and he found that he could not co-ordinate his movements. He was suffering a stroke. This was a setback for which he was entirely unprepared. There had been no premonitory symptoms, but for years he had been overstraining himself, lugging library books and tracts, tramping the precipitous terraces and alleys of Falmouth, driven by a sense of duty that overruled the protests of an ageing body. Confined to his room for two months and nursed by Jane, he spent his time reading and thinking. When he felt better, he attempted a brief walk, stopping and resting at a way-side seat, a fixture upon which he was to become increasingly dependent. He wrote a poem in praise of this amenity, invaluable for invalids, though less spectacular than the electric street lighting which was being tried out in faraway London.

But no illuminant brightened Harris's immediate prospects. He had to contend not only with illness but also with stinginess: his salary was halved during his period of recuperation. This must have caused him considerably distress, for he had previously lamented the miserliness of his ordinary wage:

> *I ask no servants livery-clad,*
>   *Or costly viands rare,*
> *Like those that crowd the rich man's board,*
>   *But simple peasant's fare –*
> *A shred of meat, a slice of bread,*
>   *Whilst feebly journeying here:*
> *Yet thou hast nought to offer me*
>   *Save thirty pounds a year.*
> (Thirty Pounds a Year)

Fate, however, seemed determined to add to his misfortune. Soon after regaining his health, he learned that Alfred, who suffered from a severe spinal disability, needed a studio to pursue his career as a photographer and engraver. Harris rated privacy higher than any earthly luxury. He was a man who sustained himself by reverie, and now after three years of blissful solitude, he felt he must abandon his hard-won cave of creation. With characteristic charity and tolerance, he said yes, let my son adapt and use my study. But Alfred's gain was the poet's loss, for he was forced out into the streets and lanes. His muse was disinherited; he was a boy again but without even a bower to shelter under.

It is a tribute to his resilience that he began a new volume of poetry, using a corner of the study for writing, but there was a detectable darkening of his mood. Time was isolating him, reducing him to the status of a lone survivor, a fact that received grim confirmation on September 17th, 1881, when, after a brief illness, his elderly mother died at Troon, Camborne. She was nursed through her last hours by her daughter of the same name and was buried at Treslothan. "A few gentle neighbours," Harris recalled, "bore her to her resting-place among the solemn pines, when the autumn leaves were falling, and the hush of twilight fell upon the earth; and at sixty-one years of age I lost the gentlest mother the world ever saw."

> *So sleep thee, mother, while I travel on*
>   *Through tears, that will not stay:*
> *Thy hand no more, as in dear seasons gone,*
>   *Can wipe those drops away.*
>
> *But oft, when Eve puts on her dusky veil,*
>   *And twilight fills the sky,*
> *Amid the mystery of the silent dale*
>   *Thy wings shall murmur by.*

It had not been an easy life for Harris's mother after the death of her husband, April 23rd 1848. The poet stated in his auto-biography that the lease of their farm reverted to the lord of the estate, William Wynne Pendarves, whose steward refused to renew it in Kitty's name, forcing her to leave, dispose of her stock and seek alternative accommodation for herself and her family. But she was not actually treated with such summary ruthlessness. After the death of John Harris Senior, Kitty was left with six children aged from 5-14 years, together with James, aged 17, and Matthew, aged 20, who actually emigrated two years later in 1850. It seems there was no one suitable to take up the leasehold and when the rent was due, on Lady Day 1849, Kitty tendered a quantity of oats valued at £4 which was accepted by the steward. The actual rent of £8-12s-6d was written off on account of the tenant being poor and the house in bad repair. It seems that Kitty had abandoned Six Chimneys by Michaelmas 1850. Taking up the tenancy of a small cottage at the bottom of the hill, she struggled on as best she could, while the farm was left untilled and unploughed for two years. Towards the end of her life, the Methodist chronicler, the Reverend Christophers, visited her and found that she looked markedly like Harris and was "evidently used to deep communings with herself and the spiritual world . . ." The poet goes further, saying how Kitty anticipated her death joyfully, when she should meet all her old friends and also see Jesus her Redeemer and Saviour.

This is the last Will and testament of me John Harris of Falmouth in the county of Cornwall.

All my real and personal estate of what nature or kind soever and wheresoever I devise and bequeath according to the nature and quality thereof to my wife Jane to and for her own absolute use and benefit.

I appoint my said wife sole executrix of this my Will and hereby revoke all wills by me heretofore made. Dated this fifteenth day of April one thousand eight hundred and seventy eight.

Signed and acknowledged by the said John Harris as his Will in the presence of us present at the same time and who in his presence and in the presence of each other all being present at the same time have hereunto subscribed our names as witnesses

John Harris

Lovell Squire
Falmouth
Jos Strudden
Clerk to
Messr Jenn & Mallen
Solr Falmouth

Jane Harris

Extract from John Harris's will signed April 1878. His personal estate, valued at £1098 14s 7d, indicates middle-class stability rather than the poverty he sometimes avowed – around £57,000 in today's money

Harris was now entering the twilight phase of his career. His health may have been impaired but creative energy still pulsed in his veins. He brought out another volume of poems, *Linto and Laneer* (1881), which was praised by a certain Mr S.C. Hall for inculcating "the higher duties of humanity – love of God, and love of man, advocating the loftiest and holiest love of both, teaching much that cannot be learned without vast profit to heart, mind, and soul." The title poem is a love story which ends with bridesmaids and wedding bells. Indebted to John Keats, the last verse echoes the *Eve of St. Agnes*:

> *The grass is green upon the stranger's grave,*
> *And Meg has passed into a higher sphere;*
> *Whilst side by side, where willow branches wave*
> *In plaintive sighs, sleep Linto and Laneer.*

But it was a sombre period for Harris despite his rigorous sense of duty. He felt the pangs of age, a weakness in his arm, palpitations and asthmatic attacks, and old friends were dying around him. As he completed his memoirs, he was distressed by the passing of Robert Alexander Grey, who had helped to distribute and sell many copies of *Wayside Pictures*. "Dear Mr Grey!" he wrote. "Even while I write this they are laying him to rest in Forest Hill Cemetery, and the muffled bells of St. Giles's are pealing his funeral dirge."

In 1882 the London firm of Hamilton, Adam and Co. brought out *My Autobiography*, a memoir concentrating on four major themes: early life, down the mine, home comforts and book-making. Harris pays tribute to the many friends who helped him along the way. There are some fine thumbnail sketches of his grandparents and an assortment of quaint and dubious local characters. The scenery of Cornwall falls across each page: the glades, meadows, daisy fields, streams and fantastic rock-piles of Carn Brea are rendered as living forms. For Harris, his birthplace was truly "Eden-odoured." But what dominates the book is the poet's self-image. His struggle is seen as something miraculous and mythical; he is the triumphal voice of poesy, breaking down the barriers of circumstance. "I was the eldest child of my parents," he began, assuming that the reader has a thoroughgoing Biblical knowledge, "who, like the smitten patriarch in the land of Uz, were blest with seven sons and three daughters." But the narrative improves after that stumbling-block opening, with vivid accounts of mining life and passages of pastoral and religious emotion; its excitable eloquence contrasts with the salt flavour of the confessional writings of that other Cornish mystic, Jack Clemo.

It was the tone of this autobiography, the element of self-idolatry, that so irritated Baring Gould. From a more tolerant standpoint, it can be seen as a disarming trait, proof of Harris's essential simplicity. A more sophisticated man would have pitched his tone more cunningly. Harris appears to be saying, "Look at me. I'm a simple, humble fellow – and a genius to boot!"

We can hazard guesses but never be entirely certain of what Harris was like as a man. No negative portrait of him exists, no letters which reflect his private side, no anecdotes from his brothers or sisters. All we are left with is his own personal testimony, portraying a modest God-fearing man blessed with a unique gift. That part of his nature was solitary, shy and retiring there can be little doubt, yet was he the model of modesty that he pretends? Could a former miner have written so voluminously and compulsively without feeling that he was a man of consequence? A great deal of his life was spent preaching, telling others how to conduct their lives. The habit of preaching is not easily abandoned and may have extended to his immediate family. One wonders, too, whether Jane Harris ever voiced her dismay when such an inordinate amount of organisation and effort went into unremunerative publishing ventures. For Harris promoted himself with exceptional vigour and somewhere, at the back of his mind, he craved large sales and recognition from the literati. When he did not get the hoped-for response, it left a bitter residue:

> *In this cold region of neglect,*
> *Perchance thou would'st have known*
> *The agony to ask for bread*
> *And only get a stone.*
> *For poverty's true friends are few,*
> *He struggles, like the mole,*
> *Who digs his tunnel in the dark,*
> *Though genius gilds his soul.*
> (The Ayrshire Ploughman)

The autobiography was well-received by the public and was later condensed and updated by James Howard Harris. In a sense, this was his last considerable achievement, an inspired account of a vanished age when religion threw out a vital lifeline to the working-man. Now little remained for Harris to do, save persevere with his mission, suffering the slings and arrows as well as the claps of encouragement. In his capacity as gospel-reader, he continued visiting houses, always striving to make mankind a little holier. Which he undoubtedly did, being a man of relentless sincerity, who refused to utilize his gifts for the wrong purpose. One day, in 1883, a gentleman asked him whether he was capable of inverting his poetic values. Could he, for instance, if he applied his resources to the task, make war seems as glorious and attractive as peace. "I could," replied Harris, "but it would not be right."

His poems continued to reflect his immediate concerns. He wrote about the loss of his little room, youthful memories, ageing, the solace of long walks and country things. One wild evening in late January, with the sea foaming and the north wind driving hail-stones, he was returning from the bed of a dying man, when he heard a robin singing and quickly dashed off a few verses. He had always liked robins; tiny, vibrant birds symbolising joyful en-durance:

> On the fence-top a sudden burst of song
> Fell strangely on my ear,
> From robin-redbreast the bare boughs among,
> Who warbled full and clear.
>
> The minstrel of the storm was hidden there
> Within a blasted tree.
> When adverse tempests strip hope's branches bare,
> O may I sing like thee.
> (A Robin-Redbreast Singing in a Storm)

Towards the end of 1883, he called on some old friends who lived in the almshouses called Earle's Retreat. While going down the stairs, he made a false step and fell backwards. He was confined indoors for several days and appeared to be recovering. Bowed, feeble and short of breath, he struggled out of bed and resumed his Bible-reading duties until December, when he was struck by an attack of spasmodic asthma. This was more serious although he maintained that the indisposition would prove temporary. Visitors called to see him and loving messages arrived daily. Christmas passed by; the poet stayed propped up in his chair; Jane and Alfred prayed for a miraculous recovery; and as he passively reclined, the clockhand advanced towards the New Year.

The dreaded asthmatic attacks came; the poet struggled but sensed he was losing ground. "Though He slay me, yet I will trust in Him," he said. On Saturday 5th January, some gentlemen and ladies came to see him. Again he affirmed his faith with the utterance:

> *"I'm a poor sinner, and nothing at all,*
> *But Jesus Christ is my All and in All."*

Two days later, on January 7th, 1884, he died in the arms of John Alfred and beside his wife. He was reclining in his arm-chair and his last utterance was "Lord! Lord!" And then, to quote his eldest son, "his soul departed from its clay tenement." In death his eye was peaceful and serene.

The funeral took place at Treslothan churchyard, a quiet tree-shaded burial ground where stark headstones stand in ranks like shields and the grass exudes a placid glow. Here Eliza Thomas had been buried and Kitty Harris almost forty years later. Nearby is the mausoleum and Gothic chapel-of-ease with its belltower and grey stones. The chapel was begun in 1840, twenty years after the poet's birth, but the setting evokes centuries of uninterrupted repose, a place of deep silence, curiously complete. If anyone had truly earned the right to that parcel of earth, it was John Harris, at last united with his beloved Lucretia in a grave bearing the epitaph – "Blessed are the peacemakers."

> *I stand like one upon a reach of elms,*
> *By the Great River's shore –*
> *Listening for voices from untrodden realms,*
> *Which thrill me evermore.*
>
> *A mystic Hand comes through the fading light*
> *Which I but dimly see*
> *And takes my lyre, and bears it out of sight,*
> *The hand that gaveth me.*
> (My Last Lay)

Take my hand.

Frontispiece from 'Last Lays' (1884)

Chapter Nineteen

Aftermath

After John Harris's death, John Lomas, previously a captain in the Salvation Army, took up the post of Scripture Reader. It is probable that the S.R.S. merged or was absorbed into the Town Mission which was still in existence in 1917.

John Alfred, assisted by Gill, issued *Last Lays* (1884) shortly after the poet's demise. The final engraver's plates show a crying Cupid and a grief-stricken woman – motifs hinting at the sadness that overlies this mild and competent collection. A feeling of slowly winding down is evident in the tribute to Longfellow, who had died two years previously. The sparse *Wearing Out* vouchsafes his love for his wife. Thoughts of boyhood revive him with memories of Forest Gate school and those early silent walks back from the mine with his father when he conjured rhymes in his head:

> *I a lad of thirteen summers,*
> *Father full and strong,*
> *Stained with ore, and dust, and sulphur,*
> *Pluto's caves among.*
>
> *Homeward three miles through all weathers*
> *He a trifle bent*
> *With the weight of tribulation,*
> *I on song intent.*

On before me, on before me,
  And no word spake he,
Till the cottage-latch was lifted,
  By the hawthorn tree.
(The Silent Walk)

Jane Harris lived on in Falmouth until 1892 when John Alfred died. Then she joined her son James Howard in Porthleven; she passed away in 1911 having reached her ninetieth year. James Howard, the eldest son, attended Exeter Diocesan Training College (the present Saint Luke's) and was appointed Master of Porthleven School, March 1878. He married Catherine Jenkin in 1881, daughter of Henry Jenkin, a farmer of Roscroggan, and they had five children: Catherine Winifred, Elizabeth Jane Mildred, Cora Millicent, Vera Jane and John Alfred. He became a lay-preacher and an occasional poet and died in 1924.

Being physically delicate, his younger brother, John Alfred, had a less happy and successful career. But we learn from his obituary that he was popular as a photographer and "well known to a large circle of friends and patrons in Penryn." He acted as librarian in the Friends' Mission Room and took an interest in the New Street Adult School which met there. He remained a bachelor and died in 1892, struck down with influenza which later developed into pneumonia. This was shortly after visiting the United States – presumably to look up his sister and uncles – and he was buried at Treslothan in the same grave as his beloved father. He possessed a slight literary gift and his best-known poem echoes his father's lament upon the death of Lucretia:

And art thou gone from us, my father dear,
  And is thy gentle, loving spirit fled?
O! thou in life we loved so well
  Art resting in thy lowly, silent bed!
And never shall we hear again
  Thy welcome tread.

Thy chair is vacant by our lonely hearth:
  Thy staff's at rest behind the study door:
Thy quill and ink are on the mantel-shelf;

But now thine earthly lays are o'er,
For thou art gone with saints to sing
On Zion's golden shore.

Concerning the appearance of the brothers, there is precious
little record. In the only photographs of them I have seen, James
Howard appears stolid and amiable with a soup-strainer
moustache, while John Alfred looks wispy, delicate, intense, like
portraits of the young Arnold Bennett.

Every so often Harris's talent is resurrected. Naturally, to
Cornish scholars such as Professor Charles Thomas, his history
and literary achievement have always been a matter of concern. Neither is Harris totally unknown: the *Dictionary of
National Biography* allows him a full entry and more recently the
late laureate Sir John Betjeman drew attention to his finer
qualities.

For the centenary of the poet's death, January 1984, a programme *Mystic Melody* was made by BBC television and D.M.
Thomas provided the commentary. "When I was born," Thomas
recalled, "the mines were derelict; though, oddly enough, the
stamps kept beating, night and day, like a heartbeat . . . the
heartbeat of a corpse on a life-support system . . . I can't tell you
what a joy it was to stumble on Harris's poetry, a poet from my
neighbourhood, my background. I knew at once this was no
bumbling local bard, but a real poet. There were lines that made
the hairs on my nape tingle . . ."

Earlier D.M. Thomas had published an article in the *Cornish
Review* along with a fine poem addressed to Harris's daughter,
Lucretia. The lines linger on the small girl dying at Christmas-
tide, "the star gliding back; the stable bare", then close in upon
the poet himself, tired and broken after a day's work, clutching
"a handful of blackberries", ending with a flooded mine, the
regenerating water of poetry:

> *bringing all he could bring*
> *you, Lucretia, his daughter,*
> *here brought you, at last, himself;*
> *he came back to Treslothan,*
> *he lay down into his love.*

The mine is filled with water;
the gift has no ending.

At Treslothan a wreath of bay leaves was placed upon the poet's grave. The Reverend Father Sutcliffe offered prayers and the wreath was laid by Charles Thomas and Richard Henry Thomas, "as the current representatives of two out of the four Bolenowe families so closely linked to John in his own lifetime." But despite such tributes, Harris's reputation has not rippled far beyond his native county. He has never been included in any national anthology of Victorian verse nor given the attention accorded to the Reverend Stephen Hawker or Sir Arthur Quiller Couch. However, Margaret Drabble has found a niche for him in her updated "Oxford Companion to Literature" and the situation is changing.

There are still many mysteries (What happened to the Shakespeare gold watch? What became of Jane Harris in America? Were all save one of the poet's notebooks destroyed?) concerning Harris and his family, many of whom emigrated to the United States. The most complete investigation into the subsequent careers of Harris's immediate family, their offspring and forebears, has been carried out by Mark Harris's grandson, Arthur Langford of Miango, Trewirgie Road, Redruth, Cornwall. If anyone reading this book has material relevant to the family, I suggest they should contact him.

PART II: THE POEMS

PART II: THE POEMS

OLD EZRA ARC.

Illustration by John Alfred Harris with printer's plate surround

Chapter Twenty

The Poetic Legacy

The virtues of the best of Harris's poetry are self-evident. It has a dense concentration, a voltaic energy, a direct emotional response, combining the apocalyptic and the homely. The poet savours the fury of the storm as much as some homely cottage parlour with a freshly sanded floor and potatoes baking in the fireside ashes. Two sides of his personality are evident in his work: the Gothic muse who broods over death, mortality and man's brutal relish for war and drink, and the affirmative spirit, who has something of the sunlit eloquence of Traherne and paints the world as a glorious spiritual revelation.

He is also good at expressing doubt and foreboding. The less emotionally secure Harris is often poetically stronger. When he was down the mine, he sensed "the hoof of fear" and the "eternal emptiness" and spoke of "some dread meaning" lurking there. The confident evangelist is silenced; terror and uncertainty reign. The best poetry often emerges from this world of thresholds and doubts.

It has been stated that Harris was finished as a poet not long after he moved to Falmouth. His job as a Scripture Reader turned him away from poetry and into the realm of tracts, hymns and verse-sermons. But the tendency was noticeable at an early stage. His first volume is full of homilies, pulpit talk and sentimentality. Harris affirmed the Victorian ethic, praising the good things of life – flowers, fields and happy families – and censuring the bad – drink, deceit and slothfulness. But he seldom railed against the society that forced him to work underground when merely a child. He was simply too childlike and ungrudging himself – an advantage when delighting in scenery or the behaviour of children, but less useful if attempting to portray psychological complexities.

Like many Victorians, though vital subject matter lay under his nose, he chose to escape into literary landscapes of the mind. Hence the specious exoticism of his Red Indian romance *Chanonchet and Wetamoe* and the relentless monotony of his Druidic pastiche "Luda". Instead of becoming the oracle of the working classes and building on impressive achievements like *Carn Brea*, he took the easy way out, retreating into the snug realms of fantasy and melodrama. In this he was like Tennyson and others who busied themselves praising Guinevere's alabaster brow or Lancelot's pristine armour while "Albion" was being transformed into an industrial slum.

What stopped him from producing work of a consistently high order was not a lack of talent so much as an inability to recognise the material of poetry. He seemed to have no astringent critic-companion to point him in the right direction or tell him when he was misusing his talent. He developed an automatic verse recipe which went something like this. First he'd fix on a name – Agnes Arrow, Peter Pine, Reuben Ross – and then he'd write a few trite rhymes around it, nailing down a moral at the end. Polished but basically effortless, such pious verses were often praised by the middle classes. Their favourite commendatory noun was "simplicity" – as though it were synonymous with merit!

The following is a selection of Harris's poems taken from the sixteen major volumes. If my treatment of his writing is slightly cavalier in its editing and abridging, I offer my apologies to the purist. Harris today is not respected for his philosophy, his lengthy morality-plays-in-verse, so much as his ability to evoke certain scenes in an arresting manner. In this abrupt culling of intensely visual lines, there is a tendency to try to promote him as an Imagist or impressionist – an idea that he would have surely resented. Yet if there is one thing that artists have no control over, it is the way in which subsequent generations will admire them.

Mining Poems

Harris spent the first half of his life underground. His mining poems have a frightening power; appalled yet fascinated, the poet contemplates the explosion-lit melodrama of his calling. Furthermore the poems contain concrete observations, technical data that anticipate Kipling, without the prettifying touches that obtrude elsewhere.

The Rescue is taken from *Wayside Pictures* and the gallant miner, who risked his life for his comrade, was Michael Verran. He was deep down in a shaft with his comrade, Jack, who had just inserted the shot for blasting. Jack tried to shorten his match by cutting it with a rock but accidentally set it alight – an explosion was imminent. The windlass-operator could not haul them both to the surface. Michael Verran said to his comrade, "Go aloft, Jack, and in one minute I shall be in heaven."

Jack went up in the bucket. The explosion followed instantly, bruising his face, and he went down again to find Verran unharmed. Miraculously the fallen rocks had formed an arch over him. The papers got hold of the story and made him a folk-hero. They learned that Verran's remarkable courage was based upon his conviction that heaven had already reserved a place for him, while he was not certain that Jack would receive the same divine consideration. (Another version – which Harris prefers – has Verran acting nobly so that Jack's family would not suffer his loss). In view of his bravery, a subscription was raised for Verran who left the mine with a grant of £50. The first thing he did was to teach himself to read and write, and then he bought some cows and took up dairy farming. He married a religious-minded milk-maid.

The extract from the long poem *The Mine* shows Harris at his evocative best. The blank verse has a breathless note-taking quality; a hectic succession of images.

The Rescue

Hast ever seen a mine? Hast ever been
Down in its fabled grottoes, walled with gems,
And canopied with torrid mineral belts,
That blaze within the fiery orifice?
Hast ever, by the glimmer of the lamp,
Or the fast-waning taper, gone down, down,
Towards the earth's dread centre, where wise men
Have told us that the earthquake is conceived,
And great Vesuvius hath his lava-house,
Which burns and burns for ever, shooting forth
As from a fountain of eternal fire?
Hast ever heard, within this prison-house,
The startling hoof of Fear? the eternal flow
Of some dread meaning whispering to thy soul?
Hast ever seen the miner at his toil,
Following his obscure work below, below,
Where not a single sun-ray visits him,
But all is darkness and perpetual night?
Here the dull god of gloom unrivalled reigns,
And wraps himself in palls of pitchy dark!
Hast ever breathed its sickening atmosphere?
Heard its dread throbbings, when the rock has burst?
Leaped at its heavings in the powder-blast?
And trembled when the groaning, splitting earth,
Mass after mass, fell down with deadliest crash?
What sayest thou? – thou hast not? – Come with me;
Or, if thou hast, no matter, come again.
Don't fear to trust me; for I have been there
From morn till night, from night till dewy morn,
Gasping within its burning sulphur-cloud,
Straining mine eyes along its ragged walls,
And wondering at the uncouth passages
Dashed in the sparry cells by Fancy's wand;
And oft have paused, and paused again, to hear
The eternal echo of its emptiness.

Come, let us leave the fields and flowers behind,
The murmuring brooklet where the poet walks,
Weaving life's cobwebs into silken flowers
To beautify the homes of fatherland.
Come, let us leave the lovely light of day,
The bower of roses, and the Muses' haunt,
Where the green ivy roofs us overhead;
And go down, down, into the earth's black breast,
Where, in the bottom of a shaft, two men
Prepare e'en now to blast the solid rock.
The hole is bored; the powder is confined;
The fuse is fixed, – it cannot be drawn forth.
They negligently cut it with a stone
Against a rod of iron. Fire is struck!
The fuse is hissing: and they fly, both fly,
Towards the bucket, taking hold thereon,
Shrieking the well-known signal. He above
Strove, but in vain, to put the windlass round.
One could escape, – delay was death to both!
One of them was our hero. Stepping back,
He looked a moment in his comrade's face, –
O what a look was that! – and cried, "Escape!
A minute more, and I shall be in heaven."
On sped the bucket up the sounding shaft:
The man was safe! Eager to watch the fate
Of his sublime deliverer, down he stooped,
And bent him o'er the shaft, just when the roar
Of the explosion rumbled from below.
Up came a fragment of the rifted rock,
And struck him on the brow, leaving a mark
Which changing time will never more efface
Till Death shall wrap him in his murky pall!

They soon began, among the fallen rock,
To burrow for the corpse. At last they heard
A cheering voice among the shining flints,
Ring in the rattling fragments! Here he was,
Roofed over with the rock, – alive and well!
Forth from his fearful grave the hero came,

And smiled on all around him. Daniel's God
Had saved His servant in this dangerous hour.
All he could tell was, that, when left alone,
He sat down in a corner of the shaft
And held a slab of stone before his eyes,
To wait the issue. And when asked why he
Gave up his life to save his friend, he said,
"His little children would be wet with grief,
While I had none but myself to mourn."

The Mine

A mine spread out its vast machinery.
Here engines with their huts and smoky stacks,
Cranks, wheels, and rods, boilers and hissing steam,
Pressed up the water from the depths below.
Here fire-whims ran till almost out of breath,
And chains cried sharply, strained with fiery force.
Here blacksmiths hammered by the sooty forge,
And there a crusher crashed the copper ore.
Here girls were cobbing under roofs of straw,
And there were giggers at the oaken hutch.
Here a man-engine glided up and down,
A blessing and a boon to mining men:
And near the spot, where many years before,
Turned round and round the rude old water wheel,
A huge fire-stamps was working evermore,
And slimy boys were swarming at the trunks.
The noisy lander by the trap-door bawled
With pincers in his hand; and troops of maids
With heavy hammers brake the mineral stones.
The cart-man cried, and shook his broken whip;
And on the steps of the account-house stood
The active agent, with his eye on all.

Below were caverns grim with greedy gloom,
And levels drunk with darkness; chambers huge
Where Fear sat silent, and the mineral-sprite

144

For ever chanted his bewitching song;
Shafts deep and dreadful, looking darkest things
And seeming almost running down to doom;
Rock under foot, rock standing on each side;
Rock cold and gloomy, frowning overhead;
Before; behind, at every angle, rock.
Here blazed a vein of precious copper ore,
Where lean men laboured with a zeal for fame,
With face and hands and vesture black as night,
And down their sides the perspiration ran
In steaming eddies, sickening to behold.
But they complained not, digging day and night,
And morn and eve, with lays upon their lips.
Here yawned a tin-cell like a cliff of crags,
And Danger lurked among the groaning rocks,
And oftimes moaned in darkness. All the air
Was black with sulphur and burning up the blood.
A nameless mystery seemed to fill the void,
And wings all pitchy flapped among the flints,
And eyes that saw not sparkled mid the spars.
Yet here men worked, on stages hung in ropes,
With drills and hammers blasting the rude earth,
Which fell with such a crash that he who heard
Cried, "Jesu, save the miner!" Here were ends
Cut through hard marble by the miners' skill,
And winzes, stopes and rizes: pitches here,
Where worked the heroic, princely tributer,
This month for nothing, next for fifty pounds.
Here lodes ran wide, and there so very small
That scarce a pick-point could be pressed between;
Here making walls as smooth as polished steel,
And there as craggy as a rended hill.

And out of sparry vagues the water oozed,
Staining the rock with mineral, so that oft
It led the labourer to a house of gems.
Across the mine a hollow cross-course ran
From north to south, an omen of much good;
And tin lay heaped on stulls and level-plots;

And in each nook a tallow taper flared,
Where pale men wasted with exhaustion huge.
Here holes exploded, and there mallets rang,
And rocks fell crashing, lifting the stiff hair
From time-worn brows, and noisy buckets roared
In echoing shafts; and through this gulf of gloom
A hollow murmur rushed for evermore.

Fall of The Old Mine Stack

Man's noblest works will fall,
  The strongest arches crack,
And Earth's proudest cities all
  Be like the old mine stack.

At February's end,
  When clouds are often black.
In storm and pelting hail
  It fell, the old mine stack.

For long, long months it shook,
  As if upon the rack,
And then it toppled o'er
  At night, the old mine stack.

We watch'd it day by day,
  Smote with the storm-king black,
Till with a solemn roar
  Down dash'd the old mine stack.

The highest peak will fall,
  Earth's mighty zones will crack,
And Nature's bulwarks all
  Be like the old mine stack.

The Streamer

The Cornish streamer was a rare old man:
Strange stories by the firelight he would tell,
When angry winds went roaring round the rocks,
And not a star looked down upon the snow.
His audience were the petted girl and boy,
And on the oak-stock's end the favourite cat.
Strange stories, bordering on the marvellous:
How once these valleys were brimful of tin,
Before King Solomon's great fane was built;
When Jews did smelt within these curious coves;
And oft a streamer's fortune had been made
By stumbling on a Jew's House wonderful;
Of giant's living in those mighty rocks,
With heaps of pearl, and waggon-loads of gold;
Of shining creatures coming from the sea,
And making poor men richer far than kings;
Of horses running swifter than the winds,
And bearing fiery comets on their backs;
Of little pixies, wearing small red cloaks,
And nightly riding timid wights to death;
Of wizards changing brands to silver bars;
Of angry dragons rolling through the air,
Uprising from old Cornwall's copper-caves.
(From Land's End)

Land's End/Kynance Cove

Travel was something Harris could seldom afford. He appears to have left Cornwall on one occasion – after winning the Shakespeare watch. But during the harvest of 1855, he visited Kynance Cove and was delighted by the sight. A year later he took his wife to Land's End and set down his impressions in letters and poems. Harris was at ease with the proud and stately manner. His conventionally pious thoughts may be a little hackneyed – "Even the grandest things decay" – but they are swamped by the rich and majestically appropriate imagery. Included here are the opening sequences of both poems.

Land's End

For me the rocks have language, and I've thought,
When gazing on these lichened chroniclers,
So stony-still, like giants clad in mail,
And slumbering on in awful dreaminess,
Of wondrous things that walk below the moon,
And feed on night-winds by the coppice-cave,
Or drink the dew from woven cups of moss,
Or dance upon the gilded lily leaves,
Or swing within the chalice of the flowers,
And glide around with golden imagery.
Now I gaze on these hoary sentinels, –
By field or fell, by castle or by cliff,
Lone in the waste, or by the village stream,
Or piled in dreadful heaps, crag over crag,
Like those around the wondrous Logan Rock,
Bare in the sunlight, dimly scanned at eve,
Tissued with moonbeams, garnished with the stars,
Or frowning 'neath the sable weeds of night, –
But tones of olden times come back again,
With dreams of song and visions of romance.

I walked the storm-swept, boulder-bound Land's End,
And mused within the sea-washed galleries,

Whose granite arches mock the rage of Time,
I revelled in the mystery of its shades,
And my soul soared up on the wings of song.
I treasured up the lore the seagulls taught,
Which in the clouds were cooing to the breeze.
I quaffed the music of this granite grove,
And read rude cantos in the book of crags,
When morn was breaking, and the lighthouse seemed
An angel in the waters, and the rocks
Rang to the music of a thousand throats.
I looked upon it as an awful poem,
Writ with the fingers of the Deity,
Whilst the proud billows of the mighty deep
Rolled on their crests the awful name of God.

Who told thee that the scenes of other lands
Were far more beautiful than aught in mine?
Who told thee that the soothing sounds of song
Fell on the ear from classic fields afar
More musical than down our thymy braes?
Who told thee that the Alps and Appenines
Had more of wildness in their very names
Than all the wonders of our Cornish coast?

Oft in my sleep I've trod the land of dreams,
And worshipped mid its still sublimity.
I've climbed the back of some dark jagged cloud,
Rolling through chaos; and methought I've heard
The breathing spirit of infinity.
I've wandered by streamlets far away,
Which seemed more musical than aught of earth;
I've travelled valleys starred with radiant flowers,
And wept upon my silent harp for joy;
I've scaled black mountains where the huge rocks rose
In grim array, a ghostly multitude,
Lifting their rough heads to the icy moon,
And shivering there in silent majesty;
And I have walked among them joyously,
Feasting my spirit on their visioned forms,

And then, awaking, wondered 'twas a dream.
But when I found me on rough Land's End,
Conning the numbers which the winds and waves
Had channelled on its pillars, not a dream
But seemed outrivalled by this craggy host.

Time plucks the coronet from kingly brows,
And scathes the laurel in the wreath of fame;
The glory of man's greatest work departs,
And o'er it drops the drapery of decay.
The hero, and the hero's blazoned deeds,
Though carved in marble, drizzled o'er with blood,
From memory fade, and shrink into the dark.
The fancy-palace built up by the bard
With its own echoes breaks and disappears;
But those eternal everlasting rocks
Sing the same cadence to the solemn sea,
And stand up strangely in their bright shell-cloaks,
With their great Maker's name upon their tongues,
As when King Arthur to the midnight marsh
Resigned the diamond-girt Excalibur.

Kynance Cove

The wondrous cliffs are polished with the waves,
And flash and flicker like huge mineral walls.
Their scaly sides are clothed with leafy gold,
And burn with beauty in the light of day.
The sands that lie on this Elysian cove
Are all ring-straked with painted serpentine:
The hollow caves the waves have fretted out
Are dashed with images of fiery hues;
And on the rocks, like beautiful psalm-leaves,
Are odes of music lovely as the light,
Trilled by the sea-nymphs in the watery robes.

I'm fond of travelling old deserted paths,
Searched by the winds and soft with solitude

Of matchless Nature in her robe of crags,
Or fringed with flowers, or edged with velvet moss;
Of grand old forests, where the trees stand up
And shout together, "God hath made us all!" –
Of odorous heaths, that oft inspire my Muse,
And lift me high on Inspiration's steep;
Of musing lonely by old Ocean's shore,
And roaming wildly through the fields of thought;
White castles, towers and palaces uprise,
Built with chaste light, and roofed with burning gems.
But starting from my song-trance one bright morn,
And turning down yon crooked curious lane,
These fancy-pictures floated in the dark,
As rock on rock uncurtained to my gaze,
And rolled upon my vision like a spell.

Hail, fairy-featured, beautiful Kynance!
A loving smile is ever on thy face,
And Beauty revels mid thy gold arcades.
Along thy glittering grottoes tones are heard
Like songs at evening by some distant lake.
Thy coloured crags, on which the sea-birds perch,
Are tuneful with the tread of tiny feet.
No harsh discordant sound is heard in thee;
And he who journeys through these sculptured creeks,
And gazes on those hills of serpentine,
Where Nature sits upon her chiselled throne,
Smiling benignly in her samphire robes,
Wearing her best, her craggy gem of crowns,
When clustered once more in his loving home,
Will feel a sweetness flowing through his heart,
And more exalted views of Nature's God.

Why seek for beauty in the stranger's clime,
When Beauty's state-room is gay Kynance?
Why seek for visions courted by the Muse?
When Kynance opens like a mine of gems?
Why seek for language from the waves' white lips
When Ocean's organ fills this pictured Cove with hymns?

Why seek for caverns striped with natural lays,
When they are stained here by the surging sea?
Why seek for islands girdled with the main,
When Kynance holds them in her feathery folds?
So mused I in the sea-damp Drawing-Room,
While through the Bellows rushed a flood of song.

Beasts and Flowers

Harris's love of nature is predominant throughout his writings. He does not view it as savage like Ted Hughes or even as sexual like D.H. Lawrence. It is wholly benevolent, as opposed to the war-making activities of men, and a fount of inspiration to the world-weary philosopher. Kindness to animals was one of his main poetic themes: "Old Golly" was Harris's faithful horse who ploughed the fields and carted the stones for the house on Troon Moor. The poem *To the Mouse* is an imitation of Harris's beloved Burns.

The gentle and accomplished wild flower verses have a measured inevitability and grace; a series of quiet, seemingly commonplace observations take on a serene radiance. Harris literally did love the wild rose – he is as thrilled by the bluebells as Wordsworth by the sight of the Ullswater daffodils. He provided the following notes to his flower poems – "Alphabetically arranged, the present collection has been composed chiefly out of doors, among the woods and streams, narrow lanes and shady paths . . . Some of these poems have been written, not so much to describe the plant named, as to become the vehicle of conveying the thought in the author's mind, which he trusts is not without its moral."

The Farmer's Apostrophe to His Old Blind Horse

And shall I turn thee out to die,
Because no light is in thy eye,
Like yon blind wretch 'neath winter's sky?
   No, eat thy oats, old Golly.

I think upon thy younger days,
When thou were all the country's praise
In cart or plough. On broad highways
   How didst thou race, old Golly!

The panting winds thou would outstrip,
Thy way through brake and bramble rip,

O'er bog and hedge, nor spur nor whip
   Dishonoured thee, old Golly.

Canst thou forget that sunny day
When thou didst draw the wain of hay
High up beyond the castle, eh?
   Thou brute of brutes, old Golly.

On market nights, astride thy back,
With my week's sirloin in my sack,
When skies were dark and lanes were black,
   Thou brought'st me home, old Golly.

But he who owns thy honest hide,
Which once shone bright in youthful pride
Will never on the common wide
   Thrust thee to die, old Golly.

So comfort thee within thy shed,
Nor fear the wild winds overhead:
I'll see that thou art housed and fed,
   Till death shall smite old Golly.

To a Mouse
(which had eaten the leaves of my lexicon)

How darest thou, soft-footed elf,
   With tiny open jaws,
To cram such crooken syllables
   Into thy greedy maw?
Would not some common household words
   Such joy to thee afford
Or crumbs that fall at supper-time
   From off our humble board?

The woodman yonder with his axe
   Looks on this book with dread,
Pronounces it an oracle

154

And shakes his hoary head.
He would not mar this mystic page,
  'Twould cripple his belief;
But thou, fur-covered sinner, com'st
  And eat'st it leaf by leaf.

What strange mice-spells thy deeds will wake,
  When in your mossy nook,
Surrounded with thy mute compeers,
  Thou talkest of my book!
Will not thy grandsire shake his head
  To hear what thou hast done?
Disturb a poet in his dreams!
  O thou degenerate son!

Take care, word-eating pilferer,
  What learned meals thou'rt at!
If I catch thee nibbling books,
  I'll give thee to the cat.
Some two-legged mice, like these, sleek rogue!
  Climb where they have no right,
Eat what belongs to other men,
  And vanish out of sight.

Jane Finding a Primrose in February

Ho, ho, pale flower, what strange mishap
Could throw thee here on Winter's lap?
Jane saw thee by the village way
  Look up with yellow eye,
'Mid cold snow-heaps that round thee lay
  Beneath a frowning sky;
And so she gathered thee, and brought
The treasure where the snows are not.

She knew the biting, blustering storm
Would rave upon thy lovely form,
And pity could not bear to see

The little stranger pale
The savage sport of Winter's glee,
    Rock'd by the frigid gale;
She could not leave thee thus alone,
And so she made thee all her own.

She deem'd the pleasant lays of Spring
From thy sweet lips were murmuring;
And as she gazed on thy wan face,
    And thought of days to come,
She pluck'd thee from thy native place,
    And bore thee to her home,
"To whisper hope" when griefs o'erpower,
And skies grow dark, and tempests lour.

Perhaps she thought sad sorrow's tear
Did on thy yellow lids appear,
And so she could not leave thee there,
    By cruel blasts defiled;
Batter'd with hail and chilling air,
    In Winter's footprint wild.
She could not leave thee 'neath such skies;
And now thou art her cherish'd prize.

If it were some unheeding boy
Who pluck'd thee in his freak of joy,
We might be angry with the lad
    Who had thus stripp'd the bower;
And it might make our bosoms sad
    To lose thee, favourite flower;
But when 'tis Jane who roams the mead,
We only love her for the deed.

Farewell, pale flower; thy reign was brief,
To see but not to savour grief,
On wintry wild to ope thine eye,
    'Mid ice and chilling sleet:
To taste the bliss of life and die
    Thus early, village sweet;

To lose thy place in Spring's loved throng,
And bloom a summer life of song.*

*The flower finds immortality or a "summer life of song" in being transformed into a poem which will be read hundreds of years later.

The Glow-Worm

The mantle of twilight was flung
   Over blossom, and beauty, and bower,
And clustering dew-beads were strung
   Upon rose-bud, and leaflet, and flower.
The moon had begun to look pale,
   The stars had lit up their bright fires,
When I hied to a brook-running vale,
   Where once was a fane of our sires.

Some rocks in the top of the dell,
   Piled wildly, looked o'er it and frowned;
Hard by was a temple, they tell,
   Whose ruins lie bleaching around.
And here, in the rifts of the storm,
   'Neath the ivy so chilly and damp,
In a bower which the woodbine did form,
   A glow-worm had lit up its lamp.

It sparkled alone in the grot,
   Like a star in calm solitude's cell;
I bore it away to my cot,
   Exulting – I loved it right well.
And long in my window 'twas found
   Emitting at evening its ray;
Shedding mystical brightness around,
   Till somebody stole it away.

Now oft, in the music of eve,
　When the curfew floats over the dale,
My cot by the river I leave,
　To wander alone in this vale.
I love, little glow-worm, to muse,
　Where the thyme with thy beauty is starred;
And I ask thee at night to diffuse
　Thy rays on the grave of the bard.

The Wild Rose

I cannot tell how it may be with others
　Over life's sandy plain,
But I have loved the hedges as my brothers
　In summer sun and rain.

And still I go to them in hours of weakness,
　When overcome with fears,
Weighed down with sorrow, and beset with bleakness,
　To weep away the tears.

But oftener do I seek their silent arches,
　As some bright vision glows,
Cheered with the whisper of the solemn larches
　And the red-rimmed WILD ROSE.

It shines among the filberts sun-surrounded,
　Smiles in the brambles drear,
Outpours its sweets where dryness long abounded,
　The beauty of the year.

Sad eyes turn to it, and they gleam for gladness;
　Care half-forgets his woes;
It has a charm for much of human sadness,
　The beautiful WILD ROSE.

The Camomile

Flower of the moor, to Nature dear,
   And sweet as thou art free,
I turn aside from crowded paths,
   To muse in peace with thee.

Thou fillest with thy pleasant smell
   The down in mosses dress'd;
The gentle breeze flows freshly by,
   And fans thy yellow vest.

The housewife loves thee, treasuring up
   Thy fragrant form with care,
Should sickness come, or wounds, or sprains;
   For thou has virtues rare.

How oft, when hands and head were tired,
   I've paced the common brown,
Or stretched me by your scented banks,
   As the great sun went down;

And heard mysterious murmurs sound
   Along the solemn sod,
The whispers of Omnipotence,
   The silent speech of God!

Dear child of Autumn, sweetest when
   The robin pipes his quill,
Along the early harvest sheaves
   Delicious camomile!

The Dodder

O'er moor paths musing, when the twilight blended
   With Eve's bright bars of red,
Came a soft sound, as the green rushes bended
   A wing-sweep overhead.

A wild bird's wing across the landscape sailing
  Where airy phantoms roam,
Or tread the moonbeams on long grasses trailing,
  Seeking his mate and home.

Yes, seeking home as darkness gently falleth
  Upon the moorland lake,
And the strange DODDER, where the fern-fay calleth
  Clings to the lonely brake.

And well that wing through twilight chambers sweeping
  Reminded me of rest,
'Neath some green hillock with the willows weeping
  And daisies o'er my breast.

Still by the red threads of the DODDER's tangle,
  Which float, or fall or cling,
Or from the upland prickly gorse-bush dangle,
  I hear that wild bird's wing.

The Bryony

The fields are full of Nature's tender teaching
  Fraught with profoundest lore
And every wild flower has a voice beseeching
  Man to revolt no more.

The summer sounds among the branches stealing
  Half jealous of release,
The wind, the rain, the solemn midnight pealing,
  Are whispering words of peace.

In the green hedgerows, where the lanes are narrow,
  None speaks to man more free,
Where chirps the wren, and cheers the noisy sparrow,
  Than the wild BRYONY.

It makes a temple of the hawthorn hoary,
  And where the alder bends:
And its red berries tell their autumn story
  When the swift rain descends.

For ever curling and for ever clinging,
  Still murmuring lays of peace;
And bidding man, while months and years are winging
  To climb, and never cease.

The Blue Bell

When the hedgerow primrose dieth,
  And the brooklet reigns
When the gentle south wind sigheth,
  Then the BLUE BELL reigns.

Waves of blue roll down the mountain,
  Swell along the lea;
Waves of blue beside the fountain,
  Where the bright maids be.

Waves of blue upon the hedges,
  By the zephyr led;
Waves of blue press by the ledges,
  Waves of blue o'erhead:

Waves of blue at every bending
  Down the village way,
Where the thatcher's song is blending
  With the linnet's lay:

Waves of blue, and sounds of singing,
  Cheat the lazy hours:
Whilst their fairy bells are ringing,
  " 'Tis the time of flowers."

Your Evangel ceaseth never
  In the year's warm youth:
Teaching man to cherish ever
  Love, and hope, and truth.

161

Lucretia Poems

Much of the best of Harris's poetry is elegiac: early death was common among miners and infant mortality was also high. The following poems lament the abrupt death of Harris's favourite daughter, Lucretia, who died at Christmas-tide, 1855; they are among the most affecting that he ever wrote. The refrain "I miss thee . . ." followed by the itemisation of the many places he delighted in sharing with her is exactly like a grief-stricken mind revolving around its point of pain. It compares with the finest elegies of the Victorian period.

On the Death of my Daughter Lucretia
(who died December 23rd, aged six years and five months)

And art thou gone so soon?
And is thy loving gentle spirit fled?
Ah! is my fair, my passing beautiful,
My loved Lucretia numbered with the dead?
Ah! art thou gone so soon?

I miss thee, daughter, now,
In the dear nooks of earth we oft have trod
And a strange longing fills my yearning soul
To sleep with thee, and be, like thee, with God!
I miss thee, daughter, now.

I miss thee at thy books,
Lisping sweet Bible-accents in my ear,
Showing me pictures by the evening lamp,
Beautiful emblems thou didst love so dear:
I miss thee at thy books.

I miss thee by the brook,
Where we have wander'd many a summer's day,
And thou wert happy with thy loving sire,
More happy here than at thy simple play:
I miss thee by the brook.

I miss thee in the Reenes,
Where we have hasted in the twilight dim
To wake the echoes of the silent dell,
And mark the glow-worm 'neath the hawthorn's limb:
   I miss thee in the Reenes.

   I miss thee on the Hill,
The dear old hill which we have climb'd so oft;
And O, how very happy we have been
In the still bower of the old heathy croft!
   I miss thee on the Hill.

   I miss thee at day's close,
When from my labour I regain my cot,
And sit down sadly at the supper-board,
Looking for thee, but, ah! I see thee not:
   I miss thee at day's close.

   I miss thee everywhere, –
In my small garden, watching the first flower, –
By the clear fountain, – in thy Sunday-class, –
Running to meet me at the evening-hour:
   I miss thee everywhere.

   Farewell my beautiful!
Thy sinless spirit is with Christ above:
Thou hast escaped the evils of the world:
We have a daughter in the meads of love.
   Farewell, my beautiful!

   When I and little Jane,
Walk hand in hand along the old hill's way,
Shall we not feel thy cherub-presence, love,
Singing our sad psalms in the twilight grey?
   I shall soon go to thee.

   Companion of the bard,
Mid rocks and trees, and hedges ivy-cross'd!
At morn and eve in Nature's presence-cell

We oft have enter'd with our musings lost,
　My child, my harp, and I.

　How thou didst love the flowers,
The mountain-heather and the buds of Spring,
The brooks and birds, the hush of solitude,
The moon and stars, like some diviner thing,
　Beautiful prophetess!

　Ah! thou were like a rose,
Dropp'd by an angel on earth's feverish clime,
To bloom full lovely, till December's winds
Blasted thy beauty in its morning prime,
　Ere it had half unclosed!

　Hush, murmuring spirit, hush!
It is the Lord, He only, who hath given:
And He hath taken – blessed be His name! –
The gem, which fell from paradise, to heaven:
　I bow and kiss His rod.

Lucretia's Grave

　'Tis where the tree-tops wave,
And gleam with glory 'neath the summer sun,
And gentle breathings steal among the boughs,
　When busy day is done.

　'Tis where a tiny rill
Glides through the silence with a trickling fall;
And ivy leaves, like holy epitaphs,
　Are clinging to the wall.

　'Tis where the grass is green,
And daisy flowers in snowy beauty lie,
And songs from fragrant field and forest screen
　Are sweetly gushing by.

'Tis where the village church
Among the dews its solemn shadow throws,
When silvery lyrics o'er the dingles float,
   At evening's gentle close.

'Tis where the weary rest,
And Age and Beauty moulder in decay;
And Hope upon the silent green sward sits,
   Watching the slumbering clay.

Above it shine the stars,
Around it woods and rocky mountains rise:
O, let it be my silent sepulchre,
   When Death has sealed mine eyes!

A Flower Gathered at Evening

Hail, blue-eyed child!
At evening mild,
I pluck thee on my native wild.

The gentle wing
Of blushing Spring,
Shook thee to the earth, thou dainty thing.

Now with shut eye
Pale dost thou lie
In twilight's dusky arms to die.

Monro

This is Harris's poetic autobiography, a fitting coda to a lifetime of writing. Although showing little of his gritty strain, his flashes of muscular power, it is quintessential Harris. Digressions sometimes overwhelm the loosely sequential narrative, but one feels that the poet poured his life into this poem, said everything that he wanted to say. It may not be his best work but it typifies him as a man. For reasons of space, this version has been extensively cut.

I

(The birth and childhood of the poet.)

He oped his eyes in the October calm,
   When every rill sang songful through the shade,
When Nature breathed her ripest, richest balm,
   And orchard-branches to the sward were weighed;
When lay-full leaves, with edges half-decayed,
   Rang song and sonnet to the rolling year,
And Beauty donned her berries in the glade,
   And voices walked the willows far and near,
And fell like old-world psalms upon the listening ear.

His gentle mother nursed her fair first-born,
   And called him Monro in her dream of joy;
And prayed for him every night and morn,
   And rocked her cradle, singing to the boy.
A bliss was hers the world could not destroy,
   Or the great clamour marching o'er the steep;
Nor Want's worn visage at the hearth annoy.
   Her love was like an angel's, pure and deep:
She hushed him when he sighed and kissed him in his sleep.

II

(Schooldays and early love of poetry.)

To school he went with satchel in his hand,
  Where sycamores o'erhung the reedy eaves,
Intent to honour the stern Dame's command,
  Clad in a bedgown with the quaintest sleeves;
Its pattern was the wain and harvest sheaves;
  She on her head a cap of muslin wore,
Which she lays by when dusky twilight leaves
  The hills with silence and the softened roar
Which summer ocean sighs on rock and fading shore.

Then first met he among the silvery streams
  And growing thyme-banks by the old hedge-stiles,
The Maid of Song, whose brow of mildness beams
  With holiest light that flows from other isles.
Entranced was he with her delicious smiles,
  And sounds that followed him from rock to rock,
Where green ferns stand in ever-graceful files,
  And moorland fairies on the moonbeams flock,
And Echo sounds her trump on every rended block.

So step by step ino the land of rhyme,
  Where hills of roses slope into the sky,
And silver waters make melodious chime,
  Young Monro wandered, though he scarce knew why;
Leaving his playmates their new toys to buy,
  Leaving his marbles treasured in their place,
Scanning the landscape with poetic eye,
  Delighted thus some bright-winged thought to chase,
Where rainbows drop their gold, and marvel at the race.

It mattered not where Monro chanced to be,
  Driving the red horse in the home-made plough,
Tending the yearlings in the clover lea,
  Or fetching the fodder for the patient cow,
Skirting the crags which stud his mountain brow,

Or school-ward creeping with his satchel green, –
His song-spray budded like a lonely bough,
    Where only waste and wildness is seen,
While here and there bright spots of herbage intervene.

When work was over, and the rake and hoe
    Were resting in the corner of the shed,
To his retreat would musing Monro go,
    And stretch himself upon some thymy bed,
While sweetly larks sang, air-hung, overhead,
    And runnels in the hollows soothed his ear,
Playing his rustic reed till daylight fled,
    And glow-worms in the dewy grass appear,
And murmurs fill the vales from some untrodden sphere.

III

(The young poet is sent down the mine.)

Then came the darkness of the dangerous mine,
    His daily, nightly tasks of tedious toil,
Where never star, or moon, or sunbeams shine,
    But sulphur-wreaths around the caverns coil,
Which health, and strength, and mental might dispoil,
    Giving the feet of time a tardy pace,
Through heated hollows and rude rifts to moil,
    When boyhood's blossom opened on his face,
And greenness clothed the tree which gave his being grace.

And what he saw, and what he suffered there,
    By day and night, can never be expressed,
Where sulphur-furies thronged the sickly air,
    And danger burrowed in the blackest vest,
Mid rocks which rent to aid his mineral-quest,
    Exploding holes, and shafts as dark as doom,
Where hollow echoes sink into the breast,
    And solemn breathings hurry through the gloom,
Like those which wizards say are murmuring from the tomb.

Sometimes his arms were heavy with his task,
  So that 'twas hard to lift them to his head,
His face like one who wore a dismal mask,
  Of black, or white, or yellow, brown, or red.
Exhausted oft, he made the flints his bed,
  And dreamt of groves of olives far away,
By dews divine and gales of gladness fed,
  Where sunlight glitters all the livelong day,
And harpers mid the trees and falling waters play.

The heat, the cold, the sulphur and the slime,
  The grinding masses of the loosened rock,
The scaling ladders, the incessant grime
  From the dank timbers and the dripping block,
The lassitude, the mallet's frequent knock,
  The pain of thirst when water was so near,
The aching joints, the blasted hole's rude shock,
  Could not dash out the music from his ear,
Or stay the sound of song which ever murmured clear.

IV

(The poet marries and raises a family.)

No church-bells rang upon his wedding-day,
  No white-robed bridesmaids by the altar stand,
No village gossips throng the public way,
  No branches wave, no lifting of the hand;
But quiet as a footfall on the sand.
  Two aged sires were all that gathered there,
The loving fathers of a different band,
  Called hence long since to breathe a purer air,
Where Heaven uplifts her towers and all is passing fair.

Then children came, like flowers, to gem his shed,
  Filling his being with a fuller joy;
In fragrant clusters round his hearth they spread,
  Whose healing odours care could not destroy;
Nor all the rigour of his rough employ:

He ran to meet them when his work was oe'r,
And kissed his girl, and danced his laughing boy,
  And gladly shared with them his simple store,
Forgetting his hard toil, and felt he was not poor.

His rhymes he wrote while they were on his knees,
  Or in the cradle sleeping by his side;
Walking abroad among the silent trees,
  Or on the mosses of the moorland wide.
They sat with him the tinkling rill beside.
  To watch the sun set o'er the bouldered steep,
And flush the brakes, and tinge the tossing tide,
  Till mystic murmurs through the dingles sweep,
And from green acorn-cups the shining fairies peep.

V

(Down in the mine, the vision of his children gives the poet
solace. One daughter [Lucretia] dies; the other [Jane] grows
up and emigrates.)

They rose before him in the gloomy shaft,
  Gleaming like angels in his fancy's eye;
And though the dregs of weariness he quaffed,
  How he would haste to meet them by-and-by!
O, had he wings, how fleetly he would fly,
  With open arms, to greet them with a kiss,
And toss them to the ceiling with a cry
  Of tenderest love, which monarchs often miss,
And feel his soul drank then more than a prince's bliss.

His good wife sat like Dorcas with her shears,
  And loved her own better than the best;
She bade her children dry their starting tears,
  And brightly look, and kept them neatly dressed;
Instilled pure Christian precepts in their breast,
  To love their neighbour and their father's friend,
And evermore to make fair Truth their guest,

And let their prayers at morn and eve ascend,
And God would be their guide and save them to the end.

When Eve came musing like a weary hind,
  And thatcher whistled down the narrow lane,
And he had left his mineral-cave behind,
  And with tired footsteps homeward walked again,
What pleasure 'twas to see them at the pane,
  With lifted hands, and faces sunned all o'er,
Waiting to feel a father's loving strain,
  And kiss him welcome at the door,
And dance their loving joys upon the white clay floor.

But they are scattered now, like husks of corn
  When the stout peasant winnows on the mead,
Feeling upon his brow the breath of morn,
  As the bright sunlight glitters on the seed.
One o'er the waters sailed with summer speed;
  And one is sleeping by the village spire,
Where the slow bells are often heard to plead
  With erring man, when Sabbath songs inspire;
And Monro now is old, and bending o'er his lyre.

VI

(The poet's love of domesticity.)

The happiest man in all the round of life,
  Is he who labours for his daily bread,
With honest hands supporting child and wife,
  Whether he earns it in the shaft or shed,
On sea or land, by chisel, plough, or thread.
  He eats his meal with blessedness untold,
And thanks his Maker with uncovered head,
  The loving shepherd of a grateful fold,
Which emperors seldom earn with all their weight of gold.

At supper-time, when sitting round the board,
  His joy was greater than the spear has won;

The jug of milk, the seed-cake from the hoard,
  And now, perchance, the pie or currant-bun.
The sands of life would then more sweetly run;
  And by his side the paper-scrap was seen,
Whereon his rustic thymes were often spun,
  Whene'er a new thought cheered his pensive mien,
Of Muses mid the springs, or lovers on the green.

His own old chair of brown unpolished elm,
  Drew him more strongly than the landlord's seat,
Where rose-buds nodded in Love's flowery realm,
  And music murmured from the tiniest feet.
He passed the drink-door in the cold and heat,
  Drawn homewards by the sunshine of his shed,
Where pure affection kept the household neat,
  Leaving no longing for bar-curtains red,
Where liquors launch their shafts till reason's self is fled.

VII

(The poet longs for release from the mine – he becomes a
Bible Reader.)

Hope never left him, though his aching limbs
  Were hanging almost like a broken bow;
But day by day he chimed his cheerful hymns
  To the pick's echo, or the river's flow:
Till from a neighbouring town, long years ago,
  Two travellers came, within the twilight still,
With faces kind, and language strong and slow,
  And told him he must leave the mining drill,
And higher, holier work for Jesus Christ fulfil.

Then he became a Reader of the Book,
  Whose every line is gilt with heavenly love,
Which tells how He our sinful nature took,
  To freely raise our ransomed souls above.
And prayed he for the meekness of the dove,
  And the Good Spirit's renovating power,

That He his feeble efforts would approve,
  And guide his erring footsteps hour by hour,
And on His precious seed the dews of mercy shower.

In hollow attics near the rended roof,
  In cellars grim, as sea-waves washed the walls,
In squalid places where peace stood aloof,
  And day and night beheld intemperate brawls,
In chambers where the obscene insect crawls,
  And lewdness burrows in a broken bed,
On wandering wights in gentle tones he calls,
  With pitying pleadings for the poor misled,
And from the Holy Book the words of life he read.

VIII

(The poet visits Stratford and the grave of Shakespeare.)

And how he felt when Stratford's glassy glades,
  And emerald meadows, burst upon his sight,
Where wicked elves still revel in the shades,
  And throng the flower-bells all the summer night,
Trooping to covert when the sun brings light,
  And mower whistles on the sloping mead,
Is not for faltering pen of mine to write;
  It should be echoed with a stronger reed,
It notes unheard before. O, he was blest indeed!

Then Monro stood above the greatest grave
  That ever human dust was known to fill;
The friend of worth, the spoiler of the knave,
  The magic wielder of the mightiest quill,
Who read the human heart with royal skill,
  And from the fields of fancy called a train
Of passing pageants, subject to his will,
  The good, the brave, the vicious and the vain,
Which no man did before, nor may create again.

His feelings in the chancel were too high
  For any finite language to repeat,
While the clear Avon murmured softly by,
  And Shakespeare's dust was lying at his feet.
He sat in silence, as it was most meet,
  While through the dim aisles solemn whispers ran,
And murmuring voices murmuring voices meet,
  And tingling chords the far-off ceiling span,
A chorus of renown to England's greatest man.

Where'er he gazed, whatever scene he saw,
  The earth, the sky, the river's shining face,
The ancient house-roofs, bending as in awe,
  Looking as if they longed to leave their place,
The wild flowers smiling with religious grace,
  The dingle-bends where gossamers entwine,
And music-shafts that strangely shoot through space,
  With all fair things that in the green reeds shine,
Held Shakespeare's name aloft, whose mission was Divine.

IX

(Back in Cornwall, the poet longs for a study to work in; he
gains it for three years, then has to relinquish it. [Harris gave
up his study for his invalid son, Alfred])

How oft he languished for the smallest fire
  Within the poorest, narrowest, loneliest cell,
Where he in peace might tune his simple lyre,
  And unmolested with his volumes dwell!
Denied him in his youth's mysterious spell,
  Denied him now when age has come at last,
And o'er the hill-tops sounds the solemn bell,
  And the last messenger approaches fast,
And hollow notes uprise upon the hurrying blast.

Three years he grasped it with a miser's joy,
  Three years it filled him with a bliss unknown,
Three years he revelled in his dear employ

174

Beneath a ceiling which he called his own;
And then a cloud from Fortune's frigid zone
  Came rolling round him in his days of pain,
And what he values most was quickly flown,
  Like rose-leaves scattered with untimely rain,
And he was forced to muse mid lanes and leas again.

X

(The poet's love of his native land.)

His native Cornwall, which his heart has worn
  Like some bright crystal in the waters clear,
Though crowding ills his soul have often torn,
  Is yet to Monro like a daughter dear.
Her hills and glens in softened light appear,
  And all her waters have a liquid sound,
Like that which fell upon his youthful ear
  When first his harp among the hills he found;
And robes of ringing rhyme her fairy form surround.

What seas of blueness does she rise between,
  Which are in thunders or deep murmurs spent!
What verse-veiled boulders from her hillocks lean,
  What tender wildings gem each craggy rent!
What landscapes green, what tors magnificent!
  What sands, and rock-birds, and dear rose-hung lanes!
What maidens smiling by the woodbined tent!
  What wives and mothers on her pasturing plains!
What crag-carved heights to chime her wild and wondrous
    strains

XI

(His task is ended . . .)

And when the pulse of life shall throb no more,
  At His command, and its red currents freeze,
When silence comes, and busy day is o'er,

Monro would sleep beneath her whispering trees,
Where sing the birds, and hum the homeward bees,
  And blush the flowers when Spring is passing by,
As notes unnumbered float upon the breeze,
  And he will watch her from the upper sky,
And at eve's musing hour will sometimes near her fly.

Farewell! farewell! A voice is in his ear,
  That time's fleet hour-glass is expending fast,
The glittering grains run faster year by year,
  With soundless drops, and soon will fall the last.
O Thou who through the gloomy grave hast past,
  Send Thy good Spirit to renew our own!
May doubt and fear for ever be outcast,
  And then uplift us to Thy glorious throne.
Where faith expands no more, and perfect love is known!

His task is ended, and he feels like one
  Whose boat is rocking 'neath the island trees,
Where gorgeous birds are fluttering in the sun,
  And harps ring sweetness on the sauntering breeze:
The hills and vales, where hum the honey bees,
  Are those he laboured to discover long,
Smiling hope-beckoned over unknown seas,
  Though fierce winds blow, and beat the billows strong.
Once more, farewell! farewell! Thus closeth Monro's song.

Sonnets

The sonnets to the months appeared in the collection *Shake-speare's Shrine*. They were praised for rendering the seasons with "Claude-like fidelity and with all the natural minuteness of John Clare." They are derivative but the more demanding rhyming scheme is welcome after the over-plangent quatrains and tripping couplets. He wrote them "each in its month" while visiting the poor of the Union workhouse, Falmouth.

June

Green fields and music. Life a cheerful bard
With song surrounded, gushing where she treads,
Comes joyous June. The great trees bow their heads
Full-leafed. On cliff and common hard
Are the marks of Summer's fingers. Beauty-starred
Are all the walks of Nature; gentle eyes
Peer out from grassy windows, and the skies
Are bridged with feathery clouds where angels glide.
Turn we to earth? The bryony and rose
In the green land are clustering side by side;
And clover-scents, in showers, are wafted wide
By village stile, and where the fountain flows
A thousand lyres ring on the gladdened plain,
Burst from the woods, and murmur from the main.

July

Heat and hay-making! Through the scented grass
The sharp scythe rustles, bringing music dear
With pastoral echoes to the listening ear;
While, in the sunshine, boy and buxom lass
Raise clover-ridges. As the gate we pass
Leading into the meadow, gales of glee
Come floating breeze-blown over lake and lea.
In the tree's shadow by the panting kine,

Rambles the angler by the limpid stream:
The earth is full of charity Divine;
Waves the green corn where glancing swallows gleam.
The lanes are loveliness where fair things dream.
A mystery fills creation. Earth and sea,
And fen, and forest, whisper, Lord, of Thee.

November

Clouds tempest-strided, heavy-sounding rain,
Wind, darkness, cold, make up thy dismal train,
Gloomy November! How the rivers rise
And echo through the hollows! Sadly flies
The last leaf through the forest whirling round,
Then hurled in anger on the sodden ground.
Sudden the change! The flowers are drowned with tears;
The pastoral field-paths, muddy, tempt no more;
The plover on the open land appears,
And little redbreast ventures near the door;
The ploughman blows his fingers by his team,
The farmer's cart rolls rumbling down the moor.
Books now, and fire, where happy faces gleam,
And cheerful chat, when day's hard toil is o'er.

December

Like the last prophet, dark December comes,
Uttering the doom of things. Hear my soul,
And profit by the teacher. List the roll
Of surging waters. Not an insect hums;
Carols no bird; cold gloom fills up the whole.
The trees, leaf-stript, lift up their arms in vain
To catch the struggling sunshine. On their steeds
The winds are mounted, prancing o'er the plain,
Then up the hills, then down the vales again.
Like a tired friend returning through the meads
He loved in childhood, after absence long,

To cheer us with the converse, even so
Comes blessed Christmas with its holy song
To gladden once again this world of woe.

Typical 'love of home' illustration by John Alfred Harris, the elaborate 'frame' was probably chosen from a selection of printers' plates

Love of Home

The romantic setting of Bolenowe and the craggy sublimities of Carn Brea were a constant source of delight to Harris. His long poem *Carn Brea* combines storm and stress with meditative passages like *Treslothan Chapel*. After a hopeful beginning, *Camborne* ends by surveying the graveyard where Harris's grandfather, father and baby sister, Anne, are buried. The *Infant Daughter Falling Asleep* shows the poet at his most relaxed; the sentimental language retains a period charm and closes with the familiar sleep-death analogy.

Treslothan Chapel

Peal on, ye gentle preachers. Day is done,
And eve steals down the vale in garments grey:
I ponder in her shadows. One sweet spot
Is ever with me, as your echoes float
Above the tree-tops, like the sweep of wings.
A little grave it is among the hills,
Beside a Gothic chapel, and I seem
To hear the tread of those who haste to prayer,
Through primrose lanes, although I'm far away.
Here I have long desired to sleep at last,
When life, with all its cares, is at an end,
Among the honest, pious villagers,
Just at the foot of my old granite mount;
That when the cottager, his day's work done,
Sits in the dusk with baby on his knee,
What time the first few tapers gild the pane,
He, listening to the river at his gate,
May think of him who carolled through his moors.

Camborne

Time chisels out the footprints of the past,
Planing away old hieroglyphic scars,
Gashing strange notches in his calendar,

And raising, on the ashes of an hour,
New wonders, to be wondrous and decay.

How like a thing of magic hast thou rose
Out of the copper-caverns of the earth,
Graceful and plain, poetically neat, –
The cottage-homes of those who work below,
Where sun, or star, or silver-margin'd cloud
Or tree, or flower, or bird, or murmuring brook,
Or chiming breeze, or tuneful waterfall,
Is never seen or heard!

I came – was led along thy narrow streets,
Stood in thy porches, heard the hum of those
Who long have slept beneath the grassy sod,
Gazed at thy toy-shop windows – gazed and gazed,
Until I thought the little horses moved,
And snapp'd their bitless bridles! then again
Rubb'd both mine eyes to see the gingerbread,
Like gilded soldiers, marching on the stall,
With lions, tigers, bears, and elephants,
And images of beasts before the Flood,
Grotesque and strange, wild, knotty, limbless things:
So that I leap'd and clapp'd my hands for joy;
And, when I sat again on mother's knee,
I thought I had realised my dream,
Had seen the very centre of the world,
And knew all bright and precious things were there,
And told her stories three or four months long.

Thou hast thy solemn grave-yard, and thy tombs,
Where lie the ashes of our pilgrim-sires,
Grass-cover'd graves, and some without a blade,
Trees weeping dew-drops at the vesper-time,
And flowers that tell all is calm below.
Here rich and poor are "huddled out of sight,"
And sweetly sleep together; not a sigh
Disturbs the halcyon of their dreamless rest!
Without its pale, a thousand voices roar

And hiss unmeaning torture! but, within,
A solemn silence sits on every bough,
And creeps with silken feet along the grass;
Voices, unseen, are whispering to the soul;
And in the tower are heard the feet of Death.
Here lie my sire and grandsire, side by side;
And here a little sister, a span long;
And I have thought, – but no, it must not be:
O let me moulder where my daughter sleeps! –
That I would hang my wild harp o'er my tomb,
And go to sleep beside them! – Fare thee well!
The silver moon unveils her lovely face,
And gazes down upon the twilight bowers,
As if she really loved thee! flinging floods
Of silver pencilling across thy robes,
And bathing thee in beauty! O 'tis sweet
Here in the moonlight to look down and see
The moonbeams dancing on the cottage-roofs!
It will be even so when we are gone,
And sleeping in our graves. – Once more, farewell!

My Infant Daughter Falling Asleep on my Knee

How softly dost thou fall asleep
Sweet cherub on my knee!
No bird can sing itself to rest
More carelessly than thee.

There's not a thought-stain on thy cheek,
Nor sorrow in thine eye;
Thou lookest like the wing of peace,
As thou asleep dost lie.

Five minutes since I heard thy song,
And stroked thy little head;
But now I lay thee down to rest
Within thy cradle-bed.

And once, my mother tells me how,
I fell asleep like thee,
Without a care-mark on my brow,
Upon my father's knee.

Sleep on, sleep on, my innocent!
When years are sped away,
O may thy rest be then as sweet
As it is now this day!

And when at last I fall asleep
In death, O, let it be
As calm and quiet as my babe's,
When slumbering on my knee.

From 'Last Lays' (1884)

Bibliography

Lays from the Mine, the Moor and the Mountain (London, 1853) (2nd ed., with additional poems, 1856)

The Land's End, Kynance Cove, and other poems (London, 1858)

The Mountain Prophet, the Mine, and other poems (London, 1860)

A Story of Carn Brea (London, 1863)

Shakespeare's Shrine (London, 1866)

Luda (London, 1868)

Bulo (London, 1871)

The Cruise of the Cutter (verse tracts; London, 1872)

Wayside Pictures (collected poems, London, 1874)

Walks with the Wild Flowers (London, 1875)

Tales and Poems (London, 1877)

The Two Giants (verse tracts, London, 1878)

Monro (London, 1879)

Linto and Laneer (London, 1881)

Last Lays (Penryn, 1884)

Biography

Gill, John *John Harris, The Cornish Poet: A Lecture on His Life and Works* (Falmouth: Alfred Harris – Penryn, J. Gill & Son), n.d. (1884) 8vo., 40 pp.

Harris, John *My Autobiography* (London: Hamilton Adams & Co. Falmouth: The Author. Penryn: John Gill and Son. Exeter: F. Clapp) (1882)

Harris, John Howard *John Harris, The Cornish Poet. The Story of His Life* (London: S.W. Partridge & Co) n.d. (1885?)

Thomas, (Antony) Charles *John Harris of Bolenowe – Poet and Preacher 1820–1884. A Tribute* (Cornish Methodist Historical Association, Occas. Publ. no. 19) (1984)

Thomas, Donald M. *Songs from the Earth. Selected Poems of John Harris, Cornish Miner, 1820-84* (Padstow: Lodenek Press) (1977)

Monk, Wendy *John Gill of Penryn* (E.J. Richard)

A few relevant articles

Rees, David "2 Poets Share Hill-Top Cottage Separated by a Century" (John Harris & Dennis Gould), *Camborne-Redruth Packet*, 31 March 1971, p. 8, illus.

Thomas, (Antony) Charles "Methodism in Cornish Literature", in: Foot, Sarah, ed., *Methodist Celebration. A Cornish Contribution* (Dyllansow Truran, Redruth), 1988; pp. 48-58 (deals strongly with John Harris).

Thomas, (Antony) Charles "Poetry at Treslothan in 1830", *Camborne Festival Magazine* (Camborne Parish Church, Nov.1973), pp. 19-23

Thomas, (Antony) Charles "The Village of Bolenowe", *Camborne Festival Magazine* (November 1982), pp.10-11

Thomas, (Antony) Charles "The Village of Bolenowe", *Journal of the Cornwall Family History Society*, 37 (Sept. 1985), pp. 18-19 (different article)

Thomas, Donald M. *Mystic Melody – John Harris, Cornish Poet and Miner 1820-84* (typescript, A4, 10 pp.) – script for a BBC/TV (Radio/TV Plymouth) programme, dated "July 1984"

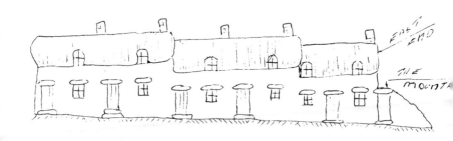

Rough drawing of Six Chimneys (John Harris's birthplace) by Arthur Langford, as it may have looked around 1840. Charles Thomas suggested that the row of five cottages had an extra chimney, but Arthur Langford quoted how the poet as a boy would spend his time sitting on "a rude arch at the end of the house" which he called 'The Mountain'. Arthur Langford comments– "I assume this to have been the front door lintel of Cottage No. 6, which had otherwise fallen down, and had originally carried Chimney No. 6."

Index